T0286087

The Conquerors

The Conquerors

How Carlo Ancelotti Made
AC Milan World Champions

Dev Bajwa

First published by Pitch Publishing, 2023

Pitch Publishing
9 Donnington Park,
85 Birdham Road,
Chichester,
West Sussex,
PO20 7AJ
www.pitchpublishing.co.uk
info@pitchpublishing.co.uk

ISBN 978 1 80150 394 5

Typesetting and origination by Pitch Publishing
Printed and bound in Great Britain by TJ Books, Padstow

Contents

Introduction

TECHNICALLY – but only by the skin of my teeth – I'm part of Generation Z. Meaning I'm old enough to remember the GameBoy Colour but young enough to not know how to get around without Google Maps.

Though much like those that came before me and the ones on the horizon, I often find myself having conversations with friends about the 'good ol' days', scoffing at the kids who appear glued to their phones, when we had to share computer privileges. It usually ends with that age-old 'remember when we were kids' conversation. True, there is some romance in how simple our lives used to be as children, as illustrated by whatever we had to keep us occupied at the time. I grew up in the era when trading cards were playground currency.

When you had to physically go into shops, glare at your parents until their wallets opened, only so you could brag and trade with your friends at breaktime. Now they have apps for all this kind of stuff – breaks my heart.

Not only do we have smaller, sleeker computer devices every ten yards from us, but general technology has advanced well beyond our understanding in only a couple of decades. Man has gone from tip-toeing on the Moon to having dreams of travelling to Mars. Modern cars, once revered for their use of internal combustion, now have the letter 'e' in front of them and get their power from the mains. And aspiring entrepreneurs now seldom find a need to navigate the murky, incestuous world of traditional media when they can record a TikTok video and hope for the best. Myself included. Search 'Dev Bajwa' for more information.

Day by day, further truth is added to the idea that anything conceivable is possible. It's exciting. It's also … extremely convenient.

Big corporations are doing everything they can to make our lives easier in return for customer loyalty. Which nobody seems to mind very much.

I'm surprised the CEO's of Deliveroo or Just Eat themselves haven't personally thanked me for my addictions, though it must be caught up along with Jeff Bezos's notice in the mail. Though even that's more digital nowadays, so maybe they just forgot!

In recent times, we've also seen a greater collective effort towards achieving a more sustainable way of living; both in the way we protect our planet and how we maintain ourselves. New-fangled ideas on 'what we should be eating' and 'what we ought to be doing' come thick and fast; such that you or I as part of that audience need only cherry-pick what sounds good and go for it. I take daily multivitamins now and have felt much better ever since. But that keto diet can run as far away from me as possible. And then, way more pertinent to the point for which all this serves as foreplay, we have content served up to us on a silver platter. Particularly when it comes to watching live sporting events or re-runs of times gone by.

The heart aches at the thought of all those key inaugural moments from the world of football that technology couldn't keep up with. We may never be able to accurately account for the number of strikes Pelé can claim, as it relies on word of mouth. The European efforts of the post-Munich Manchester United under Sir Matt Busby will continue to escape the technicolour presentation they deserve. And did Sir Geoff Hurst *really* score a legitimate decisive goal against West Germany in 1966? We may never know. Though I imagine those of the England core would prefer that particular memory remain untouched.

These days, fans rejoice at the wealth of information and material available at the flex of a fingertip. Such was my joy when growing up as a kid who could make full use of my dad's Sky Sports and TV licence portfolio.

This was back in the days when football media was a little less separated than it is now. I feel like I have to buy two used cars, insure them via a horoscope reader and complete a Spanish crossword puzzle just to watch a full weekend's worth of football. Oh, how I long for the days when ITV had the Champions League – and La Liga threw itself on to Sky every once in a while whenever the Premier League finished a bit earlier. But after things began to segregate, I must still count my lucky stars once more as new media was becoming *newer* with every passing day. Before you knew it, live streams, influencer commentary and retrospective highlight reels became more common than the games themselves.

Even now, it is rare that a day goes by when I don't watch something associated with football. And when I grow tired of the day's memes and other distasteful (yet hilarious) commentary, I like to unwind with a good, healthy dose of nostalgia.

In fact, let me check my YouTube search history right now. Which, unlike other archives, is sure to be as predictable today as any other. As it happens, here are my last five entries at the time of writing – which is the summer of 2022.

1) 'Ronaldo R9 Goal Compilation'
2) 'Thierry Henry Tribute'
3) 'Manchester United 1999 Treble Win'
4) 'Galactico Real Madrid v Barcelona'
5) 'AC Milan Best Moments'

If I'm honest, most of these videos are on loop throughout the week.

The drama. The occasions. The theatre. The passion: football at its scintillating best, and all examples I implore every modern fan to take in and appreciate while they can. Oh by the way, that last one? Don't even get me started. Actually do; that's kind of the point of this book, isn't it?

Over time, I couldn't help but develop a natural, emotive response to watching the great AC Milan side from the early 2000s. A team which alongside Manchester United, Arsenal's *Invincibles* (we'll be using that title again) and Real Madrid's *Galacticos* appeared a cut above the rest. Not only were they as successful as all great sides have to be, they possessed an aura which is difficult to force. The impact of their history reigned true in their efforts and it was like watching a new, exciting chapter to their story as it unfolded. And there we were; misty-eyed and strapped in for the ride.

The luckiest of audiences were those placed in the very arenas in which this took place. Which, regardless of how 'real' retrospective technology becomes, is an honour bestowed purely on those fortunate enough to have the stars align in that way. For those like me, we seek solace in the cold embrace of whatever camera was able to capture it; before closing our eyes and wishing we were *actually* there to make memories of our own.

Fortunately for me – when I started as an adult – it dawned on me that if I wanted to start going to games like this, I could just make it happen! A few clicks online, a number of key financial decisions later, and I could conceivably visit the very arena that played host to so many of my heroes. Granted, they wouldn't be there playing when I watched them, but I have a very active imagination. Sort of like my own *Night at the Museum* saga for the football world.

In December 2019, little ol' me looked at three very popular websites in the 'I want to go to that game' community: SkyScanner, StubHub and Trivago. Around £50 was paid out to the first for a return weekend flight to Milan from London Stansted Airport. Only half that was needed for a third-party ticket to a game between 12th-placed AC Milan and 13th-placed Sassuolo. While we are on the subject, Milan actually make it easy to get tickets directly from their personal marketplace, but I went for the cheaper option. Which made up for the lower price in grey hairs, paranoia and cold sweats. It wasn't the best decision for an overthinker like me, I have to admit. Then I was able to split the price of a hotel stay in half by sharing a twin room with a friend. Less than £100 for a football getaway? Yes please, doctor.

Kick-off was around 5pm on the Sunday (having flown out the day before); we were due to catch our flight home about six hours afterwards, so I made a point of getting there early to properly soak up everything. That was one of my better decisions. I arrived some two hours before kick-off at the Stadio do San Siro subway station, which was littered with Milan propaganda (both for AC and Inter). All presumably financed by their sponsors DAZN – for whom I was working at the time, as it turned out. After I filtered through it all and wondered which of these players on the posters I would see come the referee's first whistle, I bundled myself through those creaky turnstiles and turned my head to see where the famous San Siro stadium was. I needn't have twisted my head in any direction. It was straight ahead, standing proudly as a monument ready to come to life. It was beautiful.

Sure, there's something to be said for the grand architecture of modern stadia, but for me the romance and beauty of football comes from its history, wrapped in these grand halls which facilitated it. So, while a millennial designer might wince at the apparent simplicity of places like this (or their foundational misgivings), I find happiness in knowing that something so historic has been so beautifully preserved. Well, they're going to tear it down over the next few years, so they'll probably lose a lot of that, but still at least I got to see it and that's all that matters to me.

Upon entry, one of the ladies operating the turnstiles hoicked a scarf at my noggin which said 'AC Milan 120 Years'. It was their anniversary. I draped it round my neck and walked up a seemingly endless flight of stairs before plonking my plump rear on to my seat. A seat which incidentally was stationed a stone's throw away (or a beer can or something) from the travelling Sassuolo fans. Boded well for a nice evening, didn't it. But before things got tasty between the two sets of supporters (which they did when Milan had a goal ruled out by VAR at the beginning of the second half), the AC Milan operators treated us to a display good enough to set the wheels in motion for wanting to write this book in the first place.

To celebrate the 120-year landmark we were treated to a little light display and red carpet unveiling. 'What were they unveiling?' I hear you ask. Well, basically my childhood. Before I knew it the legends came in their droves – some of whom we'll be speaking about at length in a while. Marek Jankulovski, Massimo Ambrosini, Dida, Filippo Inzaghi, Kakha Kaladze, Clarence Seedorf. *Paolo Maldini!* Without warning, they just kept on coming and left almost as quickly; waving at the crowd and thanking us for our support before joining us on the side to watch the match. I distinctly remember Dida winking at me too. Ask him!

The match failed to live up to expectations, but that was the furthest thing from my mind. A drab 0-0 couldn't detract from the fact that I had fulfilled a lifelong dream.

I'm now able to say that I have set foot and spent a full 90 minutes in one of the greatest stadiums in the history of world football, one which represents a club I believe should be ranked in the top five or six of those ever established.

The purpose of this book is to remember the latter period of this dynasty as fondly and deservedly as its predecessors. As a matter of course, we'll briefly reminisce over Arrigo Sacchi's *Immortals* through the 80s, followed quickly by Fabio Capello's *Invincibles* of the 90s. All before the main event: one which doesn't have an official name ... until now.

Ladies and gentlemen, this is the story of Carlo Ancelotti's time as AC Milan manager, and the incredible distances over which he and his side journeyed to achieve star status. This is the story of *The Conquerors*.

CHAPTER ONE

Remembering 'The Immortals'

TO BEGIN our journey towards a period of unprecedented success for AC Milan, we need to focus on a period belonging to the opposite category.

Almost hidden among a depressingly high number of others, the club were embroiled in a scandal that would later be titled the *Totonero* affair of 1980. It was a scandal that would shine a light on an inherent problem with the way gambling in Italian sport was governed, an issue which Hamil and Morrow describe in *The governance and regulation of Italian football* (2010). It's as much a reflection on the state of Italian football at the time (one which seems to stand to this day), as it is about Italian society. They profess that there has developed a 'culture of malpractice' from a system which fails to properly dish out the appropriate punishment when necessary, thus undermining the wider public's view of the integrity of high-profile football in the country. The paradoxical allowance of and reaction to *Totonero* serves as a damning illustration of all that's broken.

For a long time, sports betting was a state-run exercise operating on a type of accumulator – allowing customers to bet on the outcome of numerous fixtures at one time from a ready-made list, and potentially seeing larger returns should all of them go their way. The process known as *Totocalcio* (soccer totaliser) was introduced in 1946 and had been immensely popular for the decades leading up to the 80s. Personally, I'm not big on betting, but I imagine it can be worth your while if you were to accurately guess the results of two or three games. Ramp that up to between ten and 12 (as per the regulations at the time) and the odds of guessing them all correctly are very slim. But so would be the stake.

From a regulatory point of view, this format's agreeable. As the aforementioned scholars (and countless others) will attest, the Italian sporting scene has had its fair share of controversies over the years. They are usually perpetuated by organised groups seeking to use their influence to affect the outcome of major events for their own gain. So, *Totocalcio* was a nifty solution to banning any nonsense for *specific* games. It would quench the public's need to gamble, even if it meant that it diminished the likelihood of a steady return. And it did work for a while.

However, as football grew in stature and fans – but let's call them 'punters' for now – enjoyed an economy affording a more comfortable lifestyle than before, the idea of seeing how well their money could work for them proved too enticing a prospect to resist against better judgement. Though, the eventual overstep didn't come from some tricky mobster looking to sink his claws into an unsuspecting perp. Instead, that honour belonged to Alvaro Trinca and Massimo Cruciani, the owner and supplier of a popular restaurant in the centre of Rome, believed to be a favoured spot for many of the Lazio representatives. From the outside it was an honest family enterprise. But within it was a sordid hunting ground with plenty of tables under which business could be done.

A couple of discounts here, maybe a vintage bottle of wine there meant the duo cultivated a position of real influence over the Lazio cohort, all before presenting their 'divide and conquer' strategy for getting around the match betting regulations. The solution was annoyingly simple: there were already a number of illegal bookmakers keen to stretch the letter of the law in their favour, and perhaps an even greater number of customers wanting to make a quick buck in such an easy way. So, if they could theoretically take control of how these fixtures would end (with the statistical method behind making the odds throwing itself from left to right with the amount of interested betters), it could be a potentially lucrative income for those now directly involved in moulding the outcome.

As a random example (not based on evidence), let's imagine that Trinca and Cruciani planned an intervention prior to Lazio playing Juventus. They look at the odds which show Juventus are heavy favourites – assuming something like giving the Rome men a 20/1 chance of overcoming the Old Lady. Obviously it would be advantageous if they could 'persuade' Juventus to throw the match. A £1,000 bet for Lazio to win would bring a £20,000 return – so multiply that by either a higher initial placement or a greater volume of gambles – and numbers may not even go as high as the one the bookmakers will owe you. It's a good plan. Very easy. Maybe a little too easy. And boundless. But completely reliant on everyone doing their part.

At the beginning, things went well for the pair as Lazio remained their focus. But the wheels fell off when they chose to expand their enterprise. Which is where AC Milan comes in. With a pretty strange outcome, it must be said.

Details of why or how are so far unannounced, but it doesn't take a genius to connect the dots. The entire issue was brought to the authorities by the very brains behind it – Trinca and Cruciani themselves. Allegedly aggrieved at the audacity of clubs not holding up to their side of the bargain, they decided to *Reverse Uno* their way into a lawsuit of their own. A kind of 'we had a deal, you broke the agreement so I'm going to tell on you' situation. I must stress that there is little evidence to better understand who were the drivers behind their decision to do this, but the punitive damages laid out by the authorities seek to paint a better picture. Cruciani held back fewer secrets than a Hayu reality show; naming a vast number of his co-conspirators in the police report. They included Giuseppe Wilson, Bruno Giordano, Massimo Cacciatori and Lionello Manfredonia of Lazio, Enrico Albertosi of AC Milan and even Paolo Rossi, of Vicenza, who was having a successful loan spell at Perugia.

Now, I'm no fraudster, but there were clear flaws in this strategy right from the beginning.

Football is a game of 11 players. Which is more than double any of the first-teamers Cruciani and Trinca were alleged to have influenced from any single club. So it's no wonder things never worked out. Only a maximum of four players were in on the ruse at any given time and, of course, they could be subbed by their unsuspecting manager or let the match pass them by if they weren't absolutely on their game. Which might not even be relevant – with the greatest of respect to them – otherwise they probably wouldn't have given in to scamming their way through a football career. Then, let's assume that things go wrong anyway and the *poliziotti* come calling. When you have enough people on your side, and operate much more smoothly than this, you're likely to keep your stories straight and work your way through an interrogation or two.

Given that it was a federal offence at the time, the punishments were severe. Many of the mentioned players received at least a three-year suspension from football – with a permanent marker against their name should they return. A further 11 players and a few club presidents were also sentenced; some of whom had the indignity of being picked off by the police before a match at their home stadium. I doubt that this was a genuine power-play to 'make an example' of the offenders, but it's a fun thought.

Very few came away from this scandal unscathed, but Paolo Rossi could have done worse. He maintained his innocence throughout the saga, but had enough information to give some evidence to the police to help clear his own name and indict others. Nevertheless, his eventual two-year suspension was an unwelcome addition to the overall 50 years' worth of sentencing that's believed to have resulted from *Totonero*. It was a suspension which was fraught with uncertainty because of his joint-ownership contract with Vicenza and Juventus. It had been arranged to give him some valuable game time at the smaller club, while remaining the asset of the bigger one.

Even with the ban, Juve saw fit to repurchase the rights to employ Rossi full-time towards the end of his banishment. It gave him just enough game time to get sharp for the upcoming 1982 FIFA World Cup in Spain. There he would become a focal point in Italy's campaign, scoring more than half their goals after an underwhelming group stage.

While Rossi was able to put the issue behind him, his more recent achivements almost completely overshadowing it, the other offenders weren't so lucky; particularly Lazio and Milan.

Both were relegated to Serie B for the new season and while Milan did get promoted back to the top division they had to do so twice before stabilising in 1983/84 when they finished sixth. They could only stand by as perennial table-toppers Juventus picked up four of a possible six post-*Totonero* titles, with prolific creator Michel Platini winning a triplet of top-scorer trophies during this time. Milan could only dream of reaching peaks like those again. All the while, the questions grew in pertinence and intensity.

When would they be able to win a *Scudetto*? Would their reputation be forever tarnished just because of a few rotten eggs? Whatever the court of public opinion would decide, one thing was for sure: to succeed they needed the right people in the right place. A solid owner – ideally with some financial muscle – a manager with good ideas on how they could get themselves back to the top, and even better players.

In 1986, one of those prayers was answered:

'Milan were in Serie B. Then I came along and promised that I would make the team the strongest in the world, but nobody believed me, not even the players.'

Silvio Berlusconi

A look at the enigma which is Silvio Berlusconi is enough to leave the average football fan with mixed feelings. Paul Ginsborg's biography, *Silvio Berlusconi: Television, Power and Patrimony*, is one of the more accurate, yet deceptively diplomatic descriptions of the enigmatic businessman and politician. Insisting that Berlusconi's story can be read as 'one part of the Milanese bourgeoisie, dynamic, parvenu and without a sense of limit, as it gains ascendancy over the other (submissive side), and in the end transforms it'. Some may call it 'brazen', 'brash' or even 'over-indulgent'; and not in a good way.

The point is, when it comes to football, all that dissipates with every moment of success you're able to bring. It's the difference between arrogance and confidence, I suppose. As an example, a player who boasts the ability of Cristiano Ronaldo without the desire to realise it but maintains they are just as good is arrogant. Cristiano, himself, is confident.

So, while Berlusconi might have been a more than eccentric figure, as polarising as he was effective, there's no escaping his ingrained positive impact on the trajectory of AC Milan after he arrived in 1986, especially following the indignation which outgoing president Giuseppe Farina had attracted.

Berlusconi's arrival, by the way, was something else.

Even now it seems too outrageous to be true. One can only presume Berlusconi was aiming to combat the negative publicity the club had attracted with a headline-grabber of his own. I suppose he was aiming to usher in his era with a spectacle befitting his promises. And I reckon he pulled it off.

Berlusconi took charge on 20 February 1986, but waited until the end of the season to introduce himself to his expectant subjects. In July of the same year, he warned the fans to brace themselves for an address on the eighth in a stadium not too far away from the San Siro, which is also known as the Giuseppe Meazza stadium depending on whether your Milanese bread is buttered red and black or blue and black. The stage Berlusconi had chosen for his arrival was the neighbouring Arena Civica, a rustic, charming, multi-purpose arena which housed Inter in the 40s. It housed a confused 10,000-strong audience waiting to see what their new owner had in store. Then, with the Sforzesco castle standing proudly in the distance, and a welcoming dance troupe warming up the crowd for the main event, Mr Silvio landed. Yes. Landed.

The man thundered through the open roof in a helicopter – propelling his way into the egos of every scorned fan who'd gone without success for so long. He even chose to have two other helicopters flown in for good measure either side of his.

It was one of those moments when you must think you're in a music video, as when there's a rainstorm outside and you watch the streams of water flow down your window. Berlusconi arrived with his own soundtrack, Wagner's *Ride of the Valkyries* blasting through the speakers.

While some may have seen it as a needlessly in-your-face stunt, about as crass as it was obvious, I (and many Milan fans of the time) disagree. From a publicity perspective it was a statement that needed to be made.

Lest we forget, it came off the back of a deeply ill-timed and shameless affair for one of the biggest clubs in the world who, incidentally, were crowned domestic champions before a couple of restaurateurs got grilled by the *Guardia di Finanza*. Milan's reputation seemed terminally affected and their squad was a far cry from rivalling clubs such as Inter and Juventus. Actually, Sky's Tomasso Fiore takes one step further in claiming that a potential audit was looming (with a devastating outcome) had they not got their act together. They were in desperate need of salvation, such that in December 1985 there was even a banner unfurled during a home game welcoming the forthcoming president when he was flirting with the idea in the press. Now, there he was, packaged like some resourceful oligarch sent from heaven, determined to restore Milan to their former glories and beyond. And he even gave the fans a taste of what was in store.

Those adjacent helicopters either side of Berlusconi served a purpose other than vanity. For, no sooner had they docked than a number of familiar faces emerged. Naturally, Franco Baresi was the first.

Now, we can argue here until we're blue in the face about who we think is the 'greatest' centre-back of all time. But we'll never come to an agreement because 'greatest' is a subjective term clouded with an objective veil, lulling us all into a false sense of security that our opinion is factual when it can't be. In reality, we each value different qualities in different ways. Most are valid, but we choose the weight, and that's a dangerous thing.

What I think we should do instead, and this is a common theme I'll choose when assessing the various players that we come across on our journey to the last page, is to make a case for things every football fan can appreciate. Baresi is a good example. He is 1.76m tall – about 5ft 9in. And he was a centre-back.

By comparison, Liverpool's Virgil van Dijk is an adonis. Tall. Strong. Fast. Handsome. Eight inches taller than Baresi. Van Dijk is the archetypal defender, and Baresi was the antithesis of pretty much all of that. Not as tall, nor as strong or quick. But Baresi was smart, *very* smart. The weird and wonderful Brazilian playmaker Zico labels him the 'consummate libero'; thereby 'capable of doing whatever he wanted with the ball whether he was defending *or* attacking'. Further testimony to his ability only seeks to confirm Zico's assessment, and converges on his positional intelligence as the reason for his success. He didn't necessarily need recovery pace to make up for a mistake, because he did not make them in the first place. And you don't need to be taller or stronger than the other guy if you're the one who gets to the ball first. He was exceptional beyond his shortcomings and wise beyond his years. All things considered it was a very sensible decision for Berlusconi to have Baresi step out of that helicopter first. After years of uncertainty, Milan could now point to their off-pitch general and their on-pitch commander. One that was 'always a Milanista' and was there to serve.

It's easy to forget that Baresi was only 26 years old as he emerged alongside Milan's new owner, but their reception told those fans everything they really needed to know about what was coming. These guys are here now. They're here to stay and they've come to play.

'I remember that day like it was yesterday. It wasn't just the helicopter ride, more the feeling that there had been this huge shift; that things really wouldn't be the same again.'

Franco Baresi

Far more than just some hot-shot who could prey on Farina's shoddy accounts, Berlusconi was a serial entrepreneur with a keen eye for making business early where others would wait; and reap the benefits thereafter. Such nous from his time with media companies Tele Milano and FinInvest was on full display in his timing to assume the Milan presidency. A new Serie A TV deal was set to kick in by the new year, so Berlusconi bided his time for an official announcement while working away in the background, focusing on polishing the club brand through its commercial arm, something he recognised as being key if he were to reclaim the aura of one of Milan's greatest assets.

Though Paris assumes the mantle for being 'The Fashion Capital of the Western World', Milan is on par with the likes of New York and London for its esteem in this area. Even during my single night's stay in 2019 I felt misplaced. There I was in my fit-for-purpose Nike hoodie and joggers set, with a Primark denim jacket draped over it for extra warmth, while my gym trainers supported me from A to B. Convenient for my vacation and perfect for the weather, but an eyesore in Milan. Everybody dressed well – even their pets – and the collective prestige of the city grew greater as we reached its epicentre: the world famous Duomo di Milano.

I got there just as golden hour cascaded over the promenade and clipped the face of the duomo. It's breathtaking. No wonder it is such a popular destination for holidaymakers. They have this man-made beauty to stare at in between retail errands at ground level. Come on, it's Milan! Of course there are shops nearby! One of which, thanks to Berlusconi, represents the loud and proud AC Milan.

It's not unlike many other club megastores that have sprouted over the years, but it was a very progressive early step for the new president. Merchandising comes in various forms, and for the average fan exceeds far beyond simply a replica shirt. An article written by Ryan Kelly at *Goal* (the media publication, not the film), explains how most teams would be lucky to receive north of ten per cent for a single shirt sold at their grounds. With most of the price – as exorbitant as it can be – being parcelled out to the many various parties involved: the sponsors, manufacturers and overhead costs to name a few. But club megastores are fulfilling demands that change every season.

Author Kevin Dixon jumps on Alan Bryman's work to make the case that more and more sectors of social and cultural life are coming to take on the manifestations of a commercial-style theme park, in what they both call the 'Disneyisation' of modern football. Playing on four key themes of adult life which lead us from our hearts straight to our wallets: (theming; hybrid consumption; emotional performative labour; merchandising). In other words, you brand something, put an idea behind it, show us why that idea makes sense and make us feel like we're part of it by giving us a piece. Berlusconi didn't have to build the San Siro from scratch, but he had a pretty major impact on making sure the rest of the journey was mapped out for us. Bryman reasons that without the theming concept, the rest is immaterial, because that's the thing that 'deems things to be made more attractive and interesting than they would otherwise be.'

While I didn't buy anything – because I was only carrying hand luggage for the flight home – I wasn't short of choice. They've got: replica shirts, retro jerseys, caps, trucker hats, hoodies, jackets, backpacks, holdalls – even a teddy bear!

The sheer scale of this enterprise takes up two floors of prime real estate in the centre of Milan (a city which comfortably asks for around $5,000 per square foot in ground rent per month), and the tills are rarely unattended. This was the first of a number of good pieces of Berlusconi business. Another was their position with the *Forza Milan* publication, a monthly magazine founded by journalist Gino Sansoni which became very popular among the *Rossoneri* faithful (both in and outside of Italy) with mail order systems long preceding the internet.

Granted, the magazine ceased to exist in June 2018, but it had a great run, chronicling the best of Milan during the most celebrated period in their history, and bringing substance to one of Berlusconi's earliest presidential proclamations, claiming: 'Milan is a team, but also a product to sell; something to offer on the market.' Obvious with hindsight, but a monumental sea-shift for the largely family-run nature of Italian football at the time. With this, AC Milan could soar higher than most with multiple income streams available to supplement their on-pitch efforts. Which is where the attention could now turn in an era that was officially saying goodbye to all things Farina.

But of course a football club can only ever be as successful as the team around which it's centred. Commercial tricks and gimmicks can only take you so far. Milan's squad needed to change.

A glance back at that side might make the Milan faithful nostalgic, particularly for some of their foreign imports; men like England's Mark Hateley and Ray Wilkins, both of whom were critically established in the football scene, and repaid their fees with a misty-eyed moment or two in red and black.

Wilkins was a tireless, internationally recognised midfielder capable of holding his own with as many flashy names as his stamina allowed. He possessed a mindset which earned him a big-money move to Milan after successful periods with Chelsea and Manchester United. However, in 1987, after three years of occasional moments and cultural struggle, he was off to Paris Saint-Germain. In the same year Hateley would also leave. I suppose the two would likely fall under 'cult hero' status, but that's nothing to be scoffed at.

Having said that, Baresi is on hand to paint a more glowing epitaph of the English pair's time at the San Siro. Admitting that 'they were big professionals, big names at the time, and they had this great optimism about them', he put their less-than-expected return down to 'bad timing'; as Milan 'were never at their best while they were there'.

Hateley's entire career seemed to run off of good form and impulse; taking him every which way to see where would be best to uncover his striker's instinct. Milan played host to some of those moments, though his time appeared best spent in Scotland and France; the latter of which came with Arsene Wenger's Monaco, of all places.

As a side note, Hateley came in to replace another Englishman, this time in the form of misfiring nomad Luther Blissett. Purchased for a princely £1 million off the back of a promotion-winning season with Watford, Blissett (perhaps to a greater degree than his replacement) struggled to adapt to the 'negative' context of Italian *calcio*, a plague which would affect more than its fair share of creative players it must be said. Worse still, Blissett's blip in form revealed a particularly distasteful reception from certain pools of the Italian media, some of whom laughably believed that Milan had had a case of mistaken identity when signing off on the Blissett deal. Also at Watford at the time, was a raw, talented winger named John Barnes, who to some commentators appeared as another 'in-form black player' who could be 'easily mistaken' with Blissett. Both players dismiss the claims – Blissett calling it 'an absolute load of nonsense' in an ITV interview around 20 years after leaving the club. Then, *The Guardian* newspaper did a little bit of digging and sought the views of Italian football journalist Gabriele Marcotti. He, as insightful and well-informed as ever, summarises: 'There are two main reasons for which I think [these allegations] are not true. First, even the most ignorant and provincial person could see that Blissett and Barnes looked absolutely nothing alike. Second, the fact is that at that time Milan were looking for an out-and-out goalscorer and Barnes just wasn't that type of player.' My trust in Marcotti's assessment and general faith in humanity considers the matter closed. Though it reveals a clear mismanagement of Milan's transfer policy.

At the time, Serie A clubs (like many domestic leagues) limited the amount of foreign players allowed on their roster. And over two seasons, almost £3 million of a dwindling pre-Berlusconi budget was wired overseas in the hope that they'd come good. Surprising, considering the modus operandi of then-manager Nils Liedholm, a pillar of Milanese history, who made a name for himself as a progressive playmaker in the 50s. Perhaps he was ahead of his time as a manager, or he was the right person at the wrong time for Milan. Not only did he have a few boastful entries on his CV in charge of Roma directly before, but the actual way he played football was encouraging to the future of an organisation like this. Italians were famous for their defensive prowess – with the employment of a sweeper between the goalkeeper and back line being more common than some tricky forward who could disrupt the opposition's version of the system. History ought to credit Liedholm with being one of the first to employ such diverse tactics into his Roma and Milan sides – prioritising positional fluidity and exciting forward movements over the boring, regressive setting he was in.

It's a shame, perhaps, that the Berlusconi revolution came during Liedholm's reign rather than before. All in time to watch his insufficient side eke out a meagre fifth-place finish in Serie A and a dissatisfying round of 16 exit from that season's Coppa Italia (the go-to domestic cup competition in Italian football). Assuming he'd had enough time to see if he was up for the task and deciding not to extend his plateauing reign any longer, the Swede was axed in April 1987 – with that cup fixture proving more critical than once feared, a 1-0 defeat to Serie B side Parma; a team led by shoe salesman-cum-manager Arrigo Sacchi.

> 'I never realised that to be a jockey you had
> to be a horse first.'
>
> *Arrigo Sacchi*

Sacchi was a very interesting character, clearly well-armed in the art of verbal combat and psychological influence as a coach. Quick-witted in the media, unafraid to take a risk and (to find a silver lining) freed from the weight of expectation attached to accomplished managers, he had done very well at Parma given where they were and what he had to work with. He had never been a professional footballer himself – hence that snarky quote above which came as a retort to allegations that he didn't possess the experience required to be successful in the role.

Even then, very few could have predicted that he would become a front-runner for the vacant managerial hot seat at AC Milan. You'd think a hot-shot like Berlusconi would want a big name to run alongside his. But Sacchi was a seducer, going into any negotiation with a superior blueprint few had the nerve to construct. Whether consciously or not, it seemed as though Sacchi sought directly to confront Milan's existing foreign transfer policy, and was able to strong-arm dissenters with a view of a brighter future without it. Funnily enough, his USP was something with which both he and Nils were enamoured; and that was the Dutch style of football that had swept the globe the previous decade, a style that was led by the late, great Johan Cruyff who was beginning to have an influence as a coach with Ajax. A style we know as *totaalvoetbal*: 'Total Football'.

Literally and simply, this form of the game meant bringing a sort of totality to the individual efforts of the playing squad, breeding players technical enough to cope with multiple situations in the game – even when they opposed their positional instincts. Tactics where a right-back wouldn't mind getting forward to whip in a cross, and the usual crosser on the wing wasn't averse to tracking back and sticking their foot in during a counter, altogether making sure that their side is attack-minded and defensive at the same time, all of the time.

Sacchi not only wanted to realise his own evaluation of this format, but to do so in a more foolproof way. I mean, what better way to establish your methods than by drafting in people who know it better than you do? Exactly. Cruyff once professed that you don't end up with the best starting 11 when you 'choose the best player from every position'. Instead, you need to cherry-pick the areas which need addressing and fine-tune your sights on to players who can fulfil them. My mind would like to place those exact words into Sacchi's mouth as he wooed Silvio into giving him the job, and foresight makes that a wonderful choice on both ends. But as with most of these things, immediate responses were different.

The press didn't take kindly to the surprise announcement of Sacchi's appointment in 1987; choosing his lacklustre coaching CV and non-existent playing career as a stick with which to beat him. That incendiary jockey quote didn't do much to get the haters off his back, but while armed with a game-plan that Berlusconi believed in – and was ready to finance – the rest, as they say, is history.

With their high defensive line, an allowance for creativity up the pitch and a press that would give Jurgen Klopp's men an asthma attack, Sacchi's AC Milan were nigh on unstoppable. All thanks to the manager's assessment of his squad and ability to take action when necessary. At the back, he inherited a line that must've been surprised to concede a shot (let alone a goal) against his Parma side the year before. A line which boasted Franco Baresi, Paolo Maldini, Mauro Tassotti and Alessandro Costacurta to name a few regulars and one which would soon bear the fruit of an effective working relationship. Roberto Donadoni was one of a number of creative players Sacchi was happy to entrust with his new strategy. But that responsibility would fall mainly on players signed as a result of Berlusconi's cheque-signing power in the transfer market.

As discussed, Hateley and Wilkins left the club upon the new coach's arrival, as he looked to find younger, more suitable replacements for his expansive style of football. Ideally, he might have hoped to find an intimidating forward who could glide into pockets of space to pick up the ball and make chances out of nothing. Then, maybe a colossus of a ball-carrying midfielder, one with immaculate control of the ball, a creative eye to thread the ball in spaces that look cordoned off and – this is pushing it now – someone with the core makeup to be a leader in the middle of the pitch. If only players like that existed …

First, Sacchi went directly to the source of all things good in the football world in search of an idea-fitting striker, and found his man in Marcel van Basten – or 'Marco' to his friends – one of the most prolific and effective front men the game has ever had the pleasure to watch.

Despite persistent ankle worries stemming from a few knocks at Ajax, the three-time Ballon d'Or-winning goalscorer was available at a snip; only £1 million. Which is where, with respect, the comparisons with Messrs Blissett and Hateley end. When limpless and operating at full capacity, few were able to keep up with the mind and movement of van Basten; where his spatial awareness and confidence in ability was usually enough to prove the cutting edge for Milan under Sacchi. As time went on – and his physical abilities diminished

– he showed a shrewd aptitude for the role of a target man. He was able to pluck the ball out of the air and make it do whatever he wanted. On a sadder and more ironic note, he recently made a statement marvelling at the modern progression of sports physiotherapy and chronic injury treatment. Pointing out that 'some players have 18 years in football', and that he was only able to get about ten at his best, with around half – or maybe fewer – of those years spent in Italy. Nevertheless, Sacchi was able to squeeze the very best out of the Dutchman while he could. So, that's half of the recruitment forecast complete. Top striker: tick. Now, on to the other one.

To run his midfield Sacchi also turned to the Netherlands in the shape of Ruud Gullit. He was a player who went above and beyond his job description for Milan. The dreadlocked Dutchman was beyond influential in realising his coach's fantasy, even if it had meant paying a record £3.5 million fee to PSV Eindhoven for the pleasure.

Together with Roberto Donadoni – a player the great Michel Platini brands as 'the best Italian footballer of the 1990s' – Gullit had free reign to establish the pace of the game, often finding himself in areas atypical to that of your average midfield 'enforcer'. Gullit was all the more encouraged by another arrival that summer, a player poached upon Liedholm's return to Roma after his sacking by Milan. No sooner had he arrived in the capital than he was made to part company with the club captain Carlo Ancelotti.

Yes, The Carlo Ancelotti. The one on the cover. But more on him later ...

Sacchi's renovation found immediate success by bringing home the *Scudetto* (Italy's top league prize) in his introductory year – the first time AC Milan had managed to win it since the gambling scandal.

A 'good job well done' for most, but a reason to strike while the iron was hot for the ever-aspirational Sacchi–Berlusconi partnership. And the UEFA European Championships during the summer of 1988 gave the pair an opportunity to scout further reinforcements. Especially with a full-force Netherlands side to keep them entertained.

De Oranje didn't disappoint, winning Euro 88 with a confident 2-0 triumph over the Soviet

Union – Gullit and van Basten the scorers. Then, with most of the world's eyes fixed upon the two outstanding players Milan already had, Milan's were attracted to the ones they hadn't been able to approach but were planning to. They needed a composed midfielder equally at home in stopping the opposition's attack as he was in starting the transition to the counter. They chose someone van Basten himself knew well from his time at Ajax.

Following the Championships and a vote of confidence from their existing Dutch crop, Sacchi was convinced that Frank Rijkaard was his man. Rijkaard was originally a central defender but Sacchi saw him as a central midfielder, the hardener of a side, the yin to Donadoni, Gullit and Ancelotti's yang. And with a combined fee of around £6 million – enough for a lock of Erling Haaland's hair nowadays – the Dutch triumvirate were in place, ready for battle.

The highlights of Arrigo Sacchi's success from this period are timeless; spotted with cameos pertaining to the talents of the men he'd recruited, dovetailed with those he was given. Combative, creative, effective. This group had it all. Come the end of Sacchi's initial four-year stay in Milan, he won six different types of trophies including – most importantly – two successive European Cups in 1989 and 1990, matching a similar achievement by Inter Milan in the mid-60s and becoming the first outfit to do so in the red and black colours of *I Rossoneri*.

Sacchi ended his Milan voyage right on top of the continental football food chain, and 'celebrated' as many great managers tend to do by choosing a tougher role. He left the San Siro in 1991 and was appointed to lead Italy. Three years later they qualified for the FIFA World Cup finals, the first for 12 years since the tournament in which Rossi's goals led them to the title. Unfortunately, when *I Azzurri* faced Brazil in the final lightning wouldn't strike twice. The final was the first time the grandest occasion of them all was settled by penalties and the now-infamous picture of the ponytailed Roberto Baggio skying the decisive penalty is one that remains a sore subject in the annals of Italian history, though on the whole, both Baggio and Sacchi are revered for their overall legacies in Italian *calcio*. And rightly so.

Arrigo Sacchi was a true visionary and proudly takes his place as one of the most forward-thinking coaches of his era. As for the team he assembled and guided between 1987 and 1991, well, they speak for themselves.

History has granted a timelessness to all of their achievements, with the value of the rebuild and its innovation adding to the legend. Over time, like most great teams, they were given a name. You'd imagine that Sacchi liked it very much; considering that he chose it as the title for a book he released in October 2021.

The Immortals. Grandiose? Yes. Applicable? Absolutely.

CHAPTER TWO

Remembering *'The Invincibles'*

ALTHOUGH SACKED by Berlusconi from the outside, Sacchi's departure left a baton heavier than Thor's hammer. (Sacchi was sacked at the end of the season and was not appointed national manager until November.)

As had been the case with most eras of similar stature, without their teacher AC Milan were at the threat of a free-fall. Fans of Arsenal and Manchester United, for example, will know exactly what that feels like. They are arguably still feeling the impact of searching for the direction and stability provided by Arsene Wenger and Sir Alex Ferguson when they departed their respective dugouts in the mid-2010s. But, staying in England, Liverpool fans (for example) will know how it feels for a new coach to come in and do just as well as – if not better than – their predecessor. Granted, few managers are as understanding, passionate and tailored to their employers as Bill Shankly and Bob Paisley were to Anfield. But homing in on somebody already well-integrated into the story of your club is a reliable way of evading teething problems. As is sticking to a historically reliable formula even if it ruffles a few feathers along the way.

So, when Arrigo Sacchi left, it would have been easy for Berlusconi and co. to try and find a like-for-like replacement; somebody already just as good as Sacchi. But no. That's exactly the kind of narrow thinking that would have stopped Sacchi getting an interview in the first place. Sacchi was an unproven manager who had the bones of a great one. He was given a chance, backed well and repaid that faith. Milan were hoping lightning would strike twice with Fabio Capello.

And it did …

Milan were more than familiar with Capello prior to offering him their managerial post. Unlike the man he was replacing Capello was a horse before becoming a jockey.

Fabio Capello enjoyed 16 years as a professional footballer – ending his boot-strapped days as a veteran holding midfielder for the *Rossoneri*. Other employers included Roma, Juventus and SPAL – with Milan keeping a keen eye on the Italian throughout his earlier stages. Liedholm was the man who was finally able to convince the mercurial middle-man to try on their colours for size, whereupon he would miss only a handful of appearances after his maiden season in 1976/77 until Father Time's cruel hand turned the tables.

Admirers of Capello are quick to point to his intelligence as a footballer, so it should come as no surprise that a coaching career was in his sights. No sooner than two years after his contract ended at Milan, he signed another – joining their *Primavera* setup in 1982. Here he made use of his education-focused two-year 'break' to oversee the success of the youth team and by 1986 put the finishing touches on his coaching qualifications. Most critically, Capello's embryonic stages as a tactician saw their practical application take place under the San Siro banner. Which, for better or worse, was a bit of a roller coaster.

Capello was there when *Totonero* blew up so he knew how detrimental it proved. In fact, he could appreciate the issue more than most – serving as a player in the run-up to their last 'wholesome' title, and helping to breed the youth prospects who were promoted to improve Milan's struggling reputation.

Berlusconi went one step further to show his support for him when he approved Capello as caretaker manager to see out the rest of the 1986/87 season once Liedholm was dismissed and before permanently appointing Sacchi. Granted, Capello was fresh out of the *Coverciano* centre when he was called up to take over for the six remaining games. It could not have been easy to fill the outgoing manager's shoes so quickly – a coach whose principles Capello outwardly admired, and to whom he owed his inauguration into top-flight management.

Capello would remain in the background while Sacchi worked his magic. Which was just as well, because the manager didn't mind plucking a few of the promising lads from the academy. So, whether he expected it or not, Capello became the focal point for fashioning talented youth products into dependable first-team regulars under Sacchi's principles. I'd imagine that, barring his players, the assistant manager and perhaps Berlusconi himself, Capello would be the one most familiar with Sacchi during his stint with *The Immortals*. Which meant he was well positioned to know how a lot of the younger guys were thinking during this time, and what was needed to fashion a proud, new-era Milan side. It was something the president must have taken into account after firing Sacchi.

Fabio Capello was reinstated as AC Milan boss on a permanent basis in June 1991 And the key question he had to answer if he was ever going to be successful was how do you improve on what Sacchi did? The data-driven newbie was ready for opening arguments.

Sacchi's final year yielded two trophies: the European Super Cup and the Intercontinental Cup, but he struggled relative to the expectations to which Milan's fanbase had grown accustomed. They finished second in Serie A behind Sampdoria, and fell out of the Coppa Italia at the semi-final stage in a boring 0-1 two-legged defeat to Roma. Then came a sacrilegious exit at the quarter-finals of the European Cup – thanks to Marseille. Top scorer Marco van Basten somehow earned that title with 11 conversions. It was far from a poor return for the departing manager, but it did go some way to relieve the weight of the mantle Capello assumed. It also gave him a blueprint on how to improve in his first year. The team was still outstanding, but maybe it needed a wee bit of stabilising.

The foundation of the squad, though brilliant, was not quite reaching its full potential under Capello early on. Nor were they as consistently together in 1990 as he intended them to be in 1991, and he addressed that.

First, he entrusted goalkeeping responsibilities to Sebastiano Rossi, giving him the first full season of an eventual 12-year career in between the Milan sticks. He averaged at least 20 league appearances in every season he spent contracted to the San Siro outfit. As far as those whose backs he'd see most of during any given 90 minutes, he couldn't have asked for a better view.

Previously, Sacchi opted to share defensive responsibilities across eight different players, with half of them bearing most of the burden, but at a staggered rate throughout the season to accommodate for European and cup commitments. Capello elected to go hell-for-leather and mostly empower only six players – the other two shared fewer than 20 matches across all competitions, who played 150 matches between them.

It's easy to consider Franco Baresi the least droppable of the back four, and he probably was, both from a seniority and experience perspective. He was viewed as the elder statesman to mentor some of the younger players Capello was choosing. As a defender, he needn't worry that Baresi was up to the task. He was 14 years into his senior Milan career and rightfully brandished the fabled *Rossoneri* captain's armband, a piece of cloth that could have equally been trusted to the player on his right; Mauro Tassotti.

Every great team has a solid utility man and Tassotti fited that bill for Milan throughout his 17 years with the club. Most of that time was spent on the right-hand side of defence, but it's folly to nail him down just as a right-back. His football intelligence and resulting versatility reminds me of Liverpool's Trent Alexander-Arnold, except, whereas the Englishman is widely considered an attacking outlet rather than a defensive specialist, Tassotti's exploits were the opposite. He didn't mind a crunching tackle or putting his body on the line to preserve the lead, and was a positional expert to ensure he was back where needed in case things didn't go to plan. He also played in defensive midfield when Capello needed him to. He was a real fighter for the Milan cause, and perennially underrated.

Stationed to the left of Tassotti and Baresi were the fresh-faced Paolo Maldini and Alessandro Costacurta. Both would emulate the best of their teachers on their own journey to greatness. Costacurta picked up versatility from Tassotti – as both were naturally adept at understanding more about the game than their position required. They realised that, if you were a good runner with a defensive mentality, you could be a full-back. But if you were also good in the air and have the patience to play the stationary game, you could be a good centre-back. Busy minds love a venture into midfield, but maturer ones are able to hold. So, to summarise Costacurta, I'd say he was an athletic, intelligent, patient ball-playing defender with a maturity beyond his years. Much like Paolo Maldini who, in my opinion, is the greatest defender I have watched. Be it through archive footage or by tracking the week-to-week progress of a player, I've yet to see anything which suggests that Maldini is anything other than the most elegant defender to have ever kicked a ball.

The Maldini name at Milan is a powerful one, spanning three generations – one either side of Paolo. His father Cesare played for 12 years and was instrumental in the growth of his son. Cesare did manage the *Rossoneri* on two separate occasions as well, but not at the right time to introduce Paolo into the Milanese line-up himself. Alerted to a name so well-renowned in the world of *I Diavolo*, the Italian press were quick to broadcast even the most tenuous link between father and son, especially when Paolo moved to a defensive full-back role from his earlier exploits as a winger.

Thankfully, this positional alteration gave Paolo an arsenal of skills that even his dad had not possessed. He was an athlete and a great one at that. Physically very fit and blessed with a mentality catered to bringing the best from that, his longevity isn't a surprise to anybody lucky enough to be associated with him.

Baresi was then a key figure in his development as a world-class centre-back; acting as an exemplar in on-pitch mentality and off-pitch professionalism. Of the two, Maldini was the sprightlier. He did like to claim the ball, march out of the back and see what his colleagues could do under pressure. But as he progressively grew under Baresi's arm, he learned to master the art of patience. Not only was he receptive to Baresi's tuition, but as a young man he welcomed it. 'He was the role model,' Maldini confirmed in an interview after his own retirement, 'he was very good with the ball' – deceptively so, perhaps. Then, tipping his hat to what's now become expected from central defenders, Maldini reasoned that Baresi's unrelenting legend in the *calcio* world was because of the difficulty 'to find a good defender who is strong and good with the ball'. So, in Maldini's world, you'd think the two were taking extra personal training sessions away from the squad to work on their 'unofficial telepathy', but Baresi's reality is different: 'He was very young, so I tried to give him some advice. But he needed very little; he was already a great player.' Whoever you believe, Capello had two professionals any manager would have dreamt of.

Together, they were the perfect pair. One wanting to impress the other, while the other felt the need to keep up with him – a great psychological contest that only benefitted Milan as the seasons came and went.

Capello also relied on his inheritance to fill that final holding midfield spot. Roberto Donadoni and Frank Rijkaard were stalwarts the next season, but Donadoni was nearing the big three-zero stage of his life and Rijkaard had already celebrated that birthday while Carlo Ancelotti was 32, the poor thing!

Capello's future-proofing strategy included, once again, promoting younger players into the starting line-up to soak up as much knowledge as they could from the elders before seeking their own path. Which, if we are to assume it worked for Maldini and Costacurta, so it did for Demetrio Albertini and his older partners.

At 20 years old, there was a lot to learn for the pimple-cheeked, battery-powered Albertini. But he was a good student. He had some first-team experience already having spent the previous season on loan at Padova and felt confident in his ability to build upon those foundations. Even Diego Fuser's arrival that summer from Fiorentina wasn't enough to dislodge a driven Albertini from that midfield berth. He soon became a focal point for the transition of the side – enjoying just over 30 appearances in the first of 11 seasons patrolling the gaps between defence and attack. Breaking up opposition play as often as he could, he would swivel on a sixpence and get on with the more positive aspects. There's a word for players like him – and the first of many idioms we'll use in this account – and that's a *regista*, which translates to 'director' in English. This role is like an impromptu orchestrator in the middle of the pitch. It needs someone who is calm, composed and thinks two or three steps ahead of the play. It took time for

Albertini to inherit these qualities, but once he did, it could make your hairs stand on end.

Thus far, the build-up of the squad showcases the tactical shrewdness and personal application of Capello's role as AC Milan manager. Many managers fall into an egotistical trap of wanting to make their new squad look like theirs. Better that, than to have whatever they achieve marred by the idea that they won something that wasn't theirs to win. So, Milan fans were able to rejoice in knowing that Capello was able to seek sense rather than personal aggrandisement. And Lady Luck rewarded his conscientiousness.

Up front, things basically went untouched. Daniele Massaro, a key, industrious though underrated figure from Sacchi's era, retained his abilities just long enough for Capello to make use of his attributes as a modern-day pressing forward.

To top it off, the mercurial van Basten escaped serious injury throughout his first season, which gave Capello arguably his best campaign since joining Milan as a coach. Van Basten was lethal without a clicky ankle to worry about. Deceptively fleet-footed for such a tall player, he was able to benefit most from the tireless work of Massaro ahead of him. After all, why should he have to track the movements of the goalkeeper and press the opposition into a mistake when there was already somebody better than him at doing it? And van Basten used Massaro's qualities to preserve his own. Those guys needed each other. And Capello knew it.

Over the course of the season, van Basten developed a knack of popping up whenever he wanted to. His first involvement came in the form of a first-minute penalty in the season's opening home win against Cagliari, and his last in a brace to complete an 8-2 thrashing away at Foggia. He scored 29 goals in all competitions that season, with 25 coming in Serie A – more than double his return in the season before Capello arrived. Gullit nearly reached double figures too. Playing alongside van Basten it was one of Ruud's best seasons from a forward's perspective. Though as admirable as Milan's goal-getting efforts were, history best remembers their impregnability at the opposite end of the pitch. Which is where we see the 'invincible' title begin to make sense.

Capello's men conceded only 25 goals in Serie A – promptly winning back the title from Sampdoria, who didn't even finish in the top five. Sampdoria also found themselves on the back end of a 5-1 dismantling at the hands of Milan in April 1992 – symbolic of the transformation the new coach was able to establish through the course of his first season. Even Albertini got on the scoresheet for that one.

As for the goals they conceded, Milan only let in more than a goal in a single game on two occasions until they let their guard down against the likes of Torino and Foggia when the season had pretty much already been tied up. As for stastistics, here's an even greater one: AC Milan did not lose a single game for the entirety of the 1991/92 domestic season. Hence, from Sacchi's *The Immortals* we now had Capello's *Invincibles*. But usually, you'd need a few years to pass before you could replicate the successes of times gone by. Not in Milan's case. Out went Sacchi, in came Capello.

They wouldn't be the only club side to earn such a soubriquet, of course. English fans hear the term Invincibles and immediately associate it with the famous Arsenal side under Arsene Wenger in 2003/04. The two top teams in Scotland have their own versions only five years apart from each other in the modern era; and we needn't even dredge up Celtic's miraculous winning-everything season with Jock Stein to keep their name in the conversation. Juventus, also – in 2011/12 – en route to that ridiculous haul of nine consecutive *Scudetti*.

However, Milan's reign remains the longest, most unexpected and largely revered tenure of them all. Not least undertaken in the toughest league in the world in their time, a league which possessed names such as Diego Maradona, Gabriel Batistuta, Gianluca Vialli and Gianfranco Zola to name but a few. Of them all, it would be Parma's Colombian hotshot Faustino Asprilla who stabbed through Milan's armour. Though it took 58 unbeaten games before he caught them napping. In this four-year period they won three successive Serie A titles and participated in the same number of European Cups.

Only when you split hairs could it be argued that the climaxes of those matches could have worked out a bit better for Capello and Milan.

Unlike in their earlier domestic success, the manager would soon no longer be able to call upon his treasured Dutch trio to do his bidding. All were beyond their prime, and Capello wasted little time in looking to the future, only that pesky 'not too many foreigners' rule forced him to rotate more than he probably would have wanted. Neither Rijkaard, Gullit nor van Basten took part in either of the last two European Cup finals, which was rebranded to the UEFA Champions League from 1992.

For the one they were involved in, they lost ignominiously, a 1-0 defeat at the hands of Marseille in 1993. It was a result steeped in controversy with the French outfit eventually being relieved of their title by UEFA having been found guilty of a number of match-fixing allegations throughout the season. Arsene Wenger, then the head coach of Monaco, remembered this in an interview with *L'Equipe* in 2006 as 'the worst period French football has been through'. He also used the word 'gangrenous' at one point; highlighting a poisonous root to all the drama which spread into surrounding and unsuspecting areas for Milan; tarnishing their game in a way they probably didn't deserve but with which they had to live.

The Marseille 'defeat' was a watershed moment for Capello and Milan. Frank Rijkaard moved back to Ajax in July 1993, while sadly the Marseille game proved to be van Basten's last for Milan. Another ankle injury caused by a hard tackle from behind by Basile Boli proved terminal.

He tried to make a comeback but the last the San Siro faithful saw of him was before the final match of the 1994/95 season, a moment which left Capello in tears. Ruud Gullit left in 1994, having missed the Champions League Final under the three foreigners rule – Capello preferring the other two Dutchmen in the starting 11 and France's Jean-Pierre Papin among the substitutes. Gullit moved to fellow title-chasers Sampdoria, initially on loan and although he returned to the San Siro briefly in 1994 he quickly went back to Sampdoria the same year.

Capello had to rebuild and three more imports led Milan to another stand-out result a year later in the Champions League Final, thus making sure that the scandal of 1993 was a Marseille problem, not theirs.

His first signing was Zvonimir Boban, a tricky Croatian winger who jinked and feinted his way to the top of Capello's wish list after six seasons with Dinamo Zagreb in which he scored 45 goals in 109 appearances. Dejan Savicevic joined a year later from Red Star Belgrade and shared the wingers' burden with fellow big-money signing Gianluigi Lentini, who was never able to quite capture the form he'd shown earlier with Torino. It is one of Italian football's most regretful 'what if' stories. In the words of his new manager, Gigi was 'a really big talent' with the required strength, will and natural ability needed to be a top winger in Serie A. Being just 23 probably played a part in his £13 million price tag which made him the most expensive player in the world. So far, it's a story we know all too well, except it wasn't poor attitude or personal application which pushed his route to the big time off course. Rather it was a crash in a Porsche 911. When driving through the outskirts of Turin in 1993 he was catapulted and the car wrecked. He returned a shell of his former self and the football world mourns the loss of a player destined to have been one of Italy's brightest wingers.

Despite this misfortune, both Boban and Savicevic did well together creatively while Capello searched to offset this with a holding midfielder to back up the maturing Albertini. He turned to the club which provided that first European final heartache. Poaching Marcel Desailly in the midst of their match-fixing investigation must have stung in France, especially given how he would help settle the score a year later. Most would have preferred a poetic reunion with Marseille, but they had been banished from that year's competition, so Capello's team had to overcome Barcelona instead. They were managed by Johan Cruyff, who had assembled a tasty side of his own, better known by another name: *The Dream Team.*

I imagine had boxing promoter Don King (or someone of that nature) been in charge of this fixture, the marketing budget would have sky-rocketed once the teams were announced. A battle for the ages. Everything on the line. Only one could win. Thankfully, the result more than lived up to expectations unless you were a Barca supporter, obviously. Right from the word go, Capello and his men looked possessed. Clearly keen to right the wrong they'd harboured from the final with *Les Olympiens*, they were ready to overcome anything that stood in the way. Tactically or otherwise.

Shrewdly, Capello understood that Barcelona possessed a fluidity that would be difficult to match man-for-man, so the team reverted to a defensive type with any Barca move forward meeting Milan's core strength. Barcelona adopted a 4-3-3 setup which meant Milan had an extra man in midfield with the wingers more inverted than usual. If anything, they looked like a 4-2-2-2 at times.

Donadoni was an attacking midfielder at heart, as was Boban but both found it easy to supplement the industry of Albertini and Desailly before they regrouped and left them to it. Funnily enough, Desailly scored the last of the four goals. There was no reply from the Catalonians.

Of all the big triumphs this was probably the single fixture most emblematic of Capello's time as AC Milan manager.

Going gung ho and abandoning a solid game plan in favour of ego and people-pleasing could have easily tipped the scales. Much like how it would have been easier to stamp his authority on his ageing squad at the beginning of his role and/or serve as the proverbial 'yes man' to Berlusconi – which is how the media had painted him upon his arrival. But he didn't let all that get to him, or at least he didn't let it show. He was a real leader and one who, despite his inexperience at the highest level, possessed an innate desire to continue where his predecessor had left off and prioritised the welfare of AC Milan above everything else in an attempt to better those achievements. Signing big players. Making bigger calls. Winning the biggest things. That was the way of his *Invincibles*.

> 'I let everyone think what they like and then I get on with the job. I let my results do the talking. I don't seek vengeance in words. My revenge comes on the pitch.'
>
> *Fabio Capello*

If the *Rossoneri* fan base felt disheartened when Sacchi left, it must have been an even bigger wrench watching Capello walk out the door in 1996. He relocated to Real Madrid in the hope of replicating his European success with the club which counts the European Cup (however it is rebranded) as their own.

Sadly, Capello would last just a single season with *Los Blancos*. Despite addressing some of the clear imbalances within their squad, he reportedly fell out with the Madrid president Lorenzo Sanz who, among other things, criticised the Italian for demoting attacking prodigy Raúl to the left wing – in order to make room for other senior players in the middle of the offensive line. Capello would return to Milan the following season, but only to find the squad disjointed and lacking confidence. He could not have imagined this would take only a year. He returned to a squad which displayed clear signs of imbalance, not helped by a poor recruitment strategy Little consideration had been paid to how various professionals would mesh with each other which was the foundation upon which the last two dynasties of Milan had been founded.

CHAPTER THREE

'I don't want to remember this'

'I have been very lucky. At least I had
ten years of a beautiful experience that
changed my life forever.'

Marco van Basten

FROM THE beginning of our timeline until now,
there were key pillars on which AC Milan had
been built. These were: trust the coach, establish
a specific playing philosophy and analyse the
positional capacity of your squad before entering
the transfer market. But in the beginning of this
Capello-free era, despite a drizzle of success here
and there, this once ultra-focused outfit turned
into a rudderless vessel.

As far as the squad was concerned, Capello had
left it in reasonable condition; still outstanding but

in need of a little polishing. With Marcel Desailly now indispensable, Capello looked to build around him. To do so, he attempted to future-proof the midfield and attack by cherry-picking two more players from the French league; Cannes' Patrick Vieira and Paris Saint-Germain's George Weah. Both on opposing ends of the experience spectrum, but hopefully with bundles of value.

But for all his promise Vieira played only twice for Milan before joining Arsenal where, of course, he became a legend. Perhaps it was too much to expect him to supplant a prime-level Desailly, an up-and-coming Massimo Ambrosini and a well-matured Demetrio Albertini?

On the other guy, I imagine few names were entered on the team sheet before George Weah. A legendary forward with a story built on a pattern of hard work and a heap of belief topped by luck. He was one of those players I would've paid top dollar to watch had I had the chance. The year he arrived – 1995 – turned out to be the highlight of his career. Not only was he crowned African Footballer of the Year for the third time (second time in a row), but he was also presented with

FIFA's coveted Ballon d'Or, bestowed upon whomsoever football's governing body deem to have had the most outstanding professional year, awarded for both his time at PSG and Milan between January and December. He arrived at the San Siro well into his prime years as a striker, but having started his professional career later than most – and hitting his potential even later than that – he could probably have added a couple more years on to his CV than what was usual. So, despite being 29, there was reasonable cause for seeing him last beyond that 30 barrier – historically the point at which managers like Capello grow tired and go on the warpath for younger alternatives. Clearly, the now-seasoned coach saw the value that remained in the Liberian. Talking to *The Irish Times* in 1996, he explained: 'Last season, we would have had as much possession, pressurised the opposition as much and created as many chances as this year, but there was no big man in the centre to finish it all. This year, there's Weah, and he puts them away.'

He did this for more than four years too, so well worth the 'risk' – had there ever been one.

I should also probably mention that they signed Roberto Baggio as well in 1995. I'll go into a little more detail about him when the time is right, but for now, let's just say that Baggio was a special player. A very special player.

It's easy to see why the football world in particular was so enamoured with him. This deft, intricate playmaker had an ability limited only by his imagination. By the time Milan registered an interest, he was 13 years a professional and already well courted by the upper echelons of the footballing community. Various reports were circulating as to why Juventus wanted to let him go, but whatever the reason, Berlusconi's persuasion was enough to prise him away from the likes of Inter, Real Madrid and Manchester United, among others, who were keeping a close eye on his situation. Thus they secured a world-class playmaker to add to their already-eye-watering levels of attacking output. He would provide ten domestic goals and 12 assists for Capello.

Milan's post-Capello dugout contained a feature from the studious Oscar Washington Tabarez. He had swapped ordering children about as a teacher to doing the same with footballers. They still lovingly call him *El Maestro* in Uruguay, probably more a mark of respect for his tenure with the national team than anything he did at club level.

Despite guiding Uruguay to some of their best competitive results in modern times, the expectation of continuing Milan's intimidating trajectory proved a burden too heavy to shoulder for Tabarez. He was relieved of his duties by December of the 1996/97 season, in the wake of a tough 3-2 away loss to Piacenza (who had to fight their way through a tie-breaker to survive relegation that season), and an 11-game streak which saw only four victories. They lost four of those too.

Looking at it objectively – and through the beautiful lens called 'hindsight' – I don't think Tabarez's recruitment choices helped him. Not for the pedigree of the players who arrived, but for the lack of wider thinking into how they would settle in. To kick things off, fate dealt him an awkward hand with an ageing group of wingers. Paulo Futre was beyond his better years, and enjoying the journeyman life far too much to be regularly available. He left for West Ham later this campaign. The great Roberto Donadoni, now 33, had earned a reprieve from the rigmarole of European football, which he aimed to find in America with the NYC MetroStars – now known as the New York Red Bulls. Then there was poor Gigi Lentini, who moved on to Atalanta in a bid to recover his pre-Milan form. He found some of it. But not all.

That left Tabarez needing – at the very least – another wide player. On top of that, a creative midfielder or competent centre-half wouldn't go amiss either. Did he tick these off? Sort of.

Jesper Blomqvist was the wide man of choice. Listening to an interview of his with two Manchester United TV presenters in 2020, I felt a sting coursing through Jesper's mic when Milan came up. He recalled a time he was asked to prepare an essay at school describing how he wanted his life to pan out. It ended up being a love letter to AC Milan and then-manager Fabio Capello, saying he would play for them one day and help them win titles. Now, as a 22-year-old promising winger, he'd be able to check off one of those three ambitions, even if he had had only three full seasons at IFK Gottenburg upon which he had to build and that pesky non-EU player rule in Serie A still limiting clubs to play a maximum of three foreign players per match, to deal with. As such, Blomqvist saw his playing time limited and re-assessing his decisions revealed that perhaps it was a a premature choice. He'd rediscover some of his confidence at Parma the next season before joining Manchester United for that fabled treble-winning campaign. So, at least he was a part of something great – even if it wasn't as he had dreamed of with Milan.

Moves for out-of-contract Ajax men Michael Reiziger and Edgar Davids proved too enticing to ignore, even if a mix of cultural teething and enforced rotation limited the pair to a joint 15-or-so starts in the league. They usually came off the bench during this period, but how often does a manager throw on a right-back (in Reiziger's case) as a gesture of good faith to change the outcome?

So, no creative midfielder or centre-back, but they did sign another foreign striker – Bordeaux's

Christophe Dugarry, someone they would have recalled as the man who knocked them out of the UEFA Cup quarter-finals the year before with a brace. He was certainly a domineering centre-forward with signs that he could go as far as the fledgling Bordeaux crop at the time. Zinedine Zidane was one of that group and that summer he went to Juventus, who held off interest from Newcastle and Blackburn, for around £3 million – less than half of what Milan shelled out for Dugarry. Now, that's not to say Dugarry was a bad player – he wasn't. But if Zidane was on Milan's radar – which it is fair to assume he was – then he should have been the focus. I think that a shrewder operator in the transfer market than Tabarez would have chosen someone more fitting to Milan's needs. Certainly one better-tuned to the way the club had behaved in the past two chapters.

Tabarez's stints on the international scene only further highlight his unsuitability to Berlusconi's project. That being said, a public statement made by the club in 2016 when 'The Teacher'was admitted to hospital to address some personal health problems, suggests that this is all water under the bridge by now.

Ignoring the single match in charge with ex-player and Tabarez assistant Giorgio Morini, history remembers a merry-go-round with two familiar faces returning to the San Siro: Arrigo Sacchi and Fabio Capello, no less.

We already know that Sacchi's reign only reached immortality when he maintained full creative control. He started a new season back then, was empowered by his president to do what he said in his interview, and the rest is history. This time, he walked into a wibbly-wobbly dressing room low on confidence having fallen so far from grace under Tabarez. The recruitment wasn't really good enough to restore any former glory and even someone of his stature struggled to keep this bucking bronco on course.

They finished 11th and exited the Champions League at the group stage. He was in charge for just 24 matches with only seven victories and seven draws. The less said about this season, the better. They sold Patrick Vieira by the way – to Arsenal.

Fabio Capello returned for the full 1997/98 season. There had been speculation that he would sign for Lazio – something their board and fan base were not best pleased about – but a return to his favourite stomping ground was his choice. Things at Real Madrid might not have gone to plan, but at least here, the theory was that he would know who he was going to be working with (from the top down), and would be well-placed to try to set the club on the right path, and to maintain the fastidious approach with which he was able to achieve that success. And he kicked things off in brutal fashion when he sold off most of Tabarez's signings – all the major ones, at least. Blomqvist went off to Parma and Edgar Davids followed quickly, adding to the Juventus ranks. Both Reiziger and Dugarry went to Barcelona, and even Roberto Baggio was shipped off to Bologna. That was possibly the biggest oversight of them all.

A roster's worth of talent on their own came in to make up the numbers. It featured big-money moves for Brazilian winger Leonardo, German utility man Christian Ziege and Senegalese winger Ibrahim Ba. Then another Ajax graduate; Patrick

Kluivert – heralded as 'the next big thing' with Weah's days numbered. They were decent players in their own right but that same year, Milan lost Baggio, Tassotti and Baresi; the first to a league rival and the others to retirement. And they weren't replaced.

Talent-wise, we know what these guys were capable of. Even today, their names rank high in most conversations relating to the history of their positions, not just in Italy, but the world. Now, they were officially exiting Milan; taking their ability and experience with them. Experience that players like Kluivert could have done with. He did still have Weah, but despite this, the pair could only muster 16 Serie A goals between them for the season. They did finish one place higher than under Tabarez and Sacchi, though – tenth.

On the whole, it's clear that Capello made an atypical mistake by not addressing the defensive problems and trying too many things too quickly. Rossi was ageing in goal and, though that's probably the only area of the pitch that gets better with age, maybe a younger improvement or, at the very least, some competition would have gone some way to elevate his performance levels. Signing the unproven Massimo Taibi didn't have the desired effect, and the youth ranks remained untouched.

Capello did move Marcel Desailly further back, which was a good move but in my opinion the manager himself showed signs of burnout. Sarah Shephard composed a thoughtful piece for *The Athletic* entitled: 'We need to talk about mental health in football', a catalogue of player and managerial exchanges pertaining to their mental wellbeing in the roller coaster football calendars. It reached the damning conclusion that more ought to be done to preserve the stability of the game's most valuable assets.

With Capello, he was reeling from the Madrid loss and keen to set the record straight. It looked like he had bitten off more than he could chew.

> 'The only regret is when I returned to Milan because I found a team that was not the team I had made.'
>
> *Fabio Capello*

Some of his players have revealed that training was uncharacteristically relaxed towards the end of the season. Milan lost six of their final nine league games, including the most damaging of defeats away at Juventus, who pumped four goals into the Milan net with just a solitary response, a Boban penalty. This served as the straw that broke the camel's back; Capello was dismissed following the Juve loss and promptly went on a year's sabbatical. He reasoned that he was missing the 'satisfaction' of management that had been present in his first stint in Milan before wishing his successor well as he stepped away.

Alberto Zaccheroni was up next. A promising stint with Udinese was enough for Berlusconi to shell out on a cross-city cab journey to discuss the Milan job in 1998. An interview soon followed, and further talks thereafter with his new board eventually committing to their biggest net spend since the season when Baggio and Weah came in. Only this time, Zaccheroni highlighted a desire to fix that shaky defence, which was a very promising start. Beginning in goal, two stoppers, Christian Abbiati and Jens Lehmann, were signed. Abbiati would outlive most of the club's later managers until he retired in 2016. Meanwhile, Lehmann returned to

Germany during the winter with his tail tucked firmly between his legs. Borussia Dortmund welcomed him with open arms, and I doubt he's looked back since.

Centre-back Bruno N'Gotty lasted a little while longer but left for Venezia on loan before the millennium ended, and then permanently to Marseille on the other side of 1999. Roberto Ayala also came and left, but lasted almost twice as long as the Frenchman and turned out to be a mighty good defender. He was a favourite of mine when he was at Valencia in La Liga. As for the attack Zaccheroni signed ex-Udinese stars Oliver Bierhoff and Thomas Helveg who were unequivocal successes under his stewardship. They stayed for a combined eight years and proved key in Milan finally reclaiming the *Scudetto* for the season. It was a massive achievement for a squad in a constant state of flux, which – as a commonly believed requisite for league success – points to the balance of the side and the forethought of their new manager in striking it.

Zaccheroni had joined a club with very little confidence in a role which looked more like a poisoned chalice with each passing season. He put his neck on the line with some risky, expensive signings in his first year in charge, probably because he knew he wouldn't get long if he didn't hit the ground running.

But Zaccheroni's successes were short-lived. That Serie A title was the only piece of silverware he'd earn at Milan in more than two and a half seasons in charge, and it would appear that stuttering form in Europe was a key contributor to Berlusconi's decision to axe his latest coach. He stated in 2001: 'I have kept my reserve about the performances [in the UEFA Champions League] because I wanted to respect the autonomy of the technical staff.' Sounds reasonable, go on. '[But] I have suffered in silence. It means I will start to take a role in the club again.'

They went on another unstable, reactionary run of operations akin to their post-Capello strategy. Mauro Tassotti was the main man for a short while who, aided by the great Cesare Maldini, did little to stem the tide. Then, Fatih Terim was given 127 days in charge on his own.

The story goes that sporting director Adriano Galliani gave the Turk the dreaded news remotely when he was home in Istanbul, apparently while the manager was delivering some sort of motivational call to a few of his players in an attempt to get some momentum for the rest of the season. Reflecting on the sacking, Terim said: 'I felt this was going to happen when the Italian championship had just started. But I am offended by the fact that they decided to sack me when I was in Istanbul without even looking into my eyes.

'The people who have self-respect never act that way. I always treat people with respect and expect from them the same.' That's a fairly reasonable, indeed tame, response for such an ending to this relationship, and I'm confident I'm not alone in condemning Terim's treatment. Maldini explained at the time, that 'as the investments rise, the club has less patience in awaiting results', and that there was 'less and less time to get things right'.

Even with the odd good moment here or there, Milan were in an undeniable free-fall. The very essence which had brought them from the depths of the *Totonero* despair to the ecstasy of European dominance had been terminally forgotten. From the boardroom, the art of trusting your manager was curtailed for a short-termism, which stunted the overall growth of the club. No real momentum could be established and if there was any it was overshadowed by the inevitability that they'd have to do it all over again. Great eras require stability above everything, and Milan were showing frightening signs of losing their footing.

Now, the ideal way forward would be to find an archetype that encapsulated the best of times gone by, but with an added ingredient of wanting to enforce their own principles for the betterment of the club's long-term future.

Not the easiest of job descriptions. And, naturally, it would take a top-class suitor to tick the right boxes. A man whose passion for the game's development was matched by their professionalism. A man who understood the impact of the past but was driven by the prospect of establishing the future.

A man like Carlo Ancelotti.

CHAPTER FOUR

'The Early Life of Carlo'

THERE ARE going to be many too-good-to-be-true moments as we journey through Carlo Ancelotti's stint as manager of AC Milan. A story of struggle, redemption and triumph, the genesis of which finds itself linked with multiple key figures featured in this book so far.

Starting at the very beginning, even Cesare Maldini gets another mention. For he was the manager at the time when a young Ancelotti was breaking through the ranks at Parma. While there, the spritely midfielder had the licence to venture further forward than would become customary in Maldini's promotion-chasing Serie C outfit. Together, they went up to Serie B in the late teen's breakthrough season. Fittingly, he made the impact which secured their progression come the end of the 1978/79 season, scoring twice in a critical play-off decider against perennial Serie C outfit Triestina. It was the first in a number of decisive moments for Ancelotti.

It seemed he somehow must have known that AC Milan was etched into his future, as he allegedly fought off very strong advances from Inter in 1979. Instead, he opted to move to an aspirational Roma side, then governed by another familiar name –Nils Liedholm. The Swede's tactically fluid methods were of great benefit to Ancelotti, both as a current player and future manager. He enjoyed a successful period with *I Giallorossi* winning the *Scudetto* in 1983. It was a treasured period of growth for Carlo, a time he remembers 'very well' and one on which he reflects with a great deal of 'fondness', the sentimental tactician still confesses that he is a 'superfan' of the club that gave him such satisfaction. In fact, long after the time-frame of this book, Ancelotti found himself on the receiving end of media reports looking to test his loyalty to then employers Chelsea. Around 2009, speculation circled around a potential return to AS Roma and naturally, he made no secret of the fact that 'I would love to return to Roma [as] it would be the only Italian club I would go to'. It's a crying shame that it never materialised.

Being from Italy's capital you'd expect the club to be impressive, bold and historic. Ancelotti agrees. In his autobiography, *Carlo Ancelotti: The Beautiful Games of an Ordinary Genius*, he lovingly describes Rome as a 'city of madness', the 'capital of [his] heart' and, most poignantly, the place where he 'learned to live'. It says a lot about his mentor, who I understand made that transition a whole lot easier.

The number of ways in which Liedholm blazed a trail during his career is bettered only by the amount of people who have good things to say about him. Elder *Milanisti* statesmen will remember him as one third of the famous 'Gre-No-Li' tripod impaling defences left and right en route to four *Scudetti* in the 50s. The other two, Gunnar Nordahl and Gunnar Gren, also went on to become managers, but tended to stay closer to their original homelands. Liedholm found a new home in Italy, and managed six different clubs there

– most on more than one occasion. Cumulatively, 12 of his post-playing years were spent in the Roma dugout across four separate spells. The second of those was where he noticed and signed Carlo Ancelotti. Well, he did have some help in this regard, it must be said, notably from Luciano Tessari and Dino Viola.

AS Roma have some pretty loud and proud digital archives, freely accessible to commoners like me. As I sifted through, I noticed Tessari's name sprinkled throughout the Liedholm era. Tessari was a goalkeeper and together their influence on Milan from the sidelines mimicked their playing careers. Liedholm, front and centre, getting all the glory and making the main decisions; Tessari, hanging about in the background, ready to answer the call. He was an assistant to Liedholm during his second period in Rome, and was apparently instrumental in having him sign off on the Ancelotti transfer. 'When Liedholm asked me what I thought, I said: "If it were up to me, I'd sign him without a doubt. In fact if I had the money I'd buy myself."' The deal still needed a man to finalise it and that man was Dino Viola, the AS

Roma president from 1979 until he sadly passed away in 1991.

> 'I'm eccentric because I'd like to do away with all formality, I'm anarchic because I detest repressive laws and I'm independent of everyone and everything, at the expense of the humblest of professions. I have deep faith and I'm very possessive of what I do, for better and for worse. I'm a free man, but not always a liberal one.'
>
> *Dino Viola*

You can infer a lot from this statement, and whichever way it speaks to you will go some way to painting a picture of Dino Viola. But there's no doubting that he was and probably always will be a treasured figure in the *Giallorossi* story. An important part of the way Viola led Milan was by establishing a viable relationship with Liedholm.

'I think I had a good relationship with him,' Viola recalls. It was certainly good enough to trust his judgement. Ancelotti's signing was just such an occasion, and backing him certainly paid off. Ancelotti played in various positions in Roma's midfield and found a school in that dressing room, learning from players like Brazilian hero Falcão. A hugely talented midfielder who helped to define what it meant to be a 'deep playmaker', it's hard to imagine that his status as an international star wouldn't have been a strong source of inspiration to those chosen alongside him. Especially so when persistent knee injuries often regressed his impact to a delegatory position on the touchline adjacent to the Roma training ground. Either way, you were either sharing a pitch or under his eye. Both he and Ancelotti were regularly available and instrumental in Roma's *Scudetto* title-winning season – a full 41 years since they had last won.

Further steady development led to Ancelotti inheriting the captaincy at the club from a different Swedish manager. Liedholm had left for AC Milan in 1984 with his place being taken by future England manager Sven-Göran Eriksson.

'I feel honoured and proud to be a part of the AS Roma Hall of Fame. The club and its atmosphere are something I'll always keep in my heart. A big thanks to all the fans and coaches that have kept me in their thoughts and who still remember me so fondly. All the best.'

Carlo Ancelotti signing off on his Hall of Fame induction

Like most good things, Carlo Ancelotti's time at Roma came to an end in 1987. By which point, he'd made quite a substantial positional transformation. He was still a midfielder but a far cry from the runaway who liked to nip in behind defenders and get on the scoresheet. Now, he was all about protecting his own goal, getting the ball in deeper areas to transition it through the thirds. He was pretty good at it, too. His abilities were deserving of more than that solitary *Scudetto* he and Roma achieved during his time there. However, if he was ever going to win more than that, he'd have to join an impressive setup. He found one.

Arrigo Sacchi was the man who prised Carlo Ancelotti from Roma and in doing so his recruit remains among the elite few who can claim to be key members of both definable eras in Milan's history. Both as a fixture of *immortality* and a foundational element of those *Invincibles*.

Ancelotti was 28 years old by the time he draped on the Milan shirt, and his ability was evident almost from the moment he was introduced. In a relatively modern interview with *FourFourTwo* – by which point, he'd grown to have a real appreciation for all things tactical and 'getting things to gel' – he remembered that Milan side as a 'really, really fantastic team', aided by playing for a manager 'who knew exactly what he wanted'. That was for his players to 'express themselves' on the pitch wherever possible and work out any off-pitch problems between them without the need for senior intervention. It was an early lesson in the art of conflict resolution so keenly observed and stored in Carlo's bulging memory bank.

He explained that communication and decision-making was the real USP to that team. Sacchi's tactical discipline tended to station Ancelotti closer to the back than the front, where I'm sure Baresi, Costacurta and the like were ready with calm and steady assessments of what needed to be done in reactive situations. Proactively, he had players like van Basten with which to natter. Van Basten, allegedly and unofficially, rewrote

Ancelotti's job description as he made the 'number six role' his own. It was something along the lines of know when I'm running and don't waste your energy to find me. Which van Basten enjoyed regularly as he found the passer in celebration when he got on the end of one of their many moves together.

'I chose the right time to go to Milan, didn't I?' said Ancelotti. He could say that again.

After Sacchi, Capello's version of Ancelotti was almost completely divorced from the forwards and best suited to allowing Milan to dictate the pace of the match from the first and second thirds. His mentorship of the incoming Demetrio Albertini was a factor, too – over time they grew to be fairly similar players – and the team benefited from the mix of youthful and mature physical and mental qualities. You simply cannot embark on runs of consistency like Milan managed without the presence of senior, experienced players like Carlo Ancelotti to keep things steady, nor can you excel in midfield when energies like Albertini's need charging. It's just a shame that his knees began to give way, and that Parma's Faustino Asprilla had to halt the run.

Altogether, the playing version of Ancelotti was a mixture of the key components of his managers. He had the unmatched thoughtfulness of Liedholm, the elder statesman-like maturity of Eriksson, the bare-faced viscosity of Sacchi. The unbridled confidence of Capello. He absorbed it all to help on his journey into management.

On that note, Sacchi would continue to guide Ancelotti by thrusting him into the Italian national team setup. It no doubt served a dual purpose, both aiding Ancelotti and inspiring his side. Ancelotti assisted his mentor as the team went on that famous run in the 1994 World Cup. Baggio error aside, it was a great field trip. And a priceless educational experience.

Upon completion of his full coaching qualifications at Coverciano (the technical headquarters of the Italian Football Federation) in 1995 Serie B side Reggiana would be the first to sample what Ancelotti could provide. It was an auspicious step for a man Sacchi once described as his 'coach on the pitch'. Reggiana needed something fresh, and Ancelotti needed an opportunity. Leaning on inspired goalscorer Alfredo Aglietti, Reggiana

THE EARLY LIFE OF CARLO

earned immediate promotion to Serie A by 1996. No sooner had they gone up than Parma came calling. It was a steep step up for any manager after their first full coaching season in professional football, but Ancelotti has always been aspirational. So for him, progressing to a club with greater facilities and ambition was a necessary challenge. There's a quote by Benjamin Franklin, one of the Founding Fathers of the US, that would probably resonate with Ancelotti – 'Without continual growth and progress, such words as improvement, achievement, and success have no meaning.'

Additionally, with his status as a welcome ex-player and the club's own roster of young, exciting talent, I doubt it took long for Ancelotti to pack his bags and move back to Parma. Hindsight is wonderful, but look at these names: Gianfranco Zola, Enrico Chiesa, Hristo Stoichkov, Lilian Thuram, Gianluigi ('Gigi') Buffon, Fabio Cannavaro, Hernán Crespo. All at different stages of their own careers, sure but who would not want to work with players of that stature?

Early on, Ancelotti found difficulty in making enough space for the sheer wealth of options he had at his disposal – especially when banking on a system not too dissimilar to the one he'd seen under Sacchi. Though there was a freedom in the way the creative players were emboldened to forge opportunities, the system itself was clear: 4-4-2.

Four tough, uncompromising defenders, a balance of one 'enforcer' and one 'creator' in central midfield. Then flying, tricky playmakers deployed wide plus either a target man or a pressing forward to complement a more complete striker. As you'd imagine, Chiesa and Crespo had little difficulty adapting to their new manager's request, nor did Cannavaro or Buffon. But for others, among them Gianfranco Zola, implementing a system like this was the kiss of death.

A natural trickster with a penchant for putting on a show, Zola was a master of his craft, ready to feed off of any defensive insecurities he could sniff out, always provided he was afforded the opportunity to be free from positional prohibition. As eloquently described by future manager Claudio Ranieri, 'Gianfranco tries everything because he is a wizard and the wizard must try.' Cute but pertinent when you consider what happens to him when he isn't allowed to 'try'.

Needless to say, Zola found his creativity stifled by the inherent rigidity of a typical 4-4-2, because he didn't really fit into any of the roles Ancelotti looked to use. As the only forward player on the left-hand side (the area which appeared most suitable to complement Zola's right foot), he needed to hold his position, resist the counter and not go gung-ho for fear of alienating his left-back. A younger Stoichkov used to do this very well – especially as part of that Barcelona *Dream Team* later in his career – and showed glimpses of his marauding magic as he approached the 30 barrier before re-joining Barca the next season.

For now, this overall tactical fit displaced Zola, who found his spiritual home at Chelsea; a plucky, transitioning club which was all too happy to let him do whatever he wanted, provided he kept a smile on his face and encouraged the fans to do the same. He did just that, and the smile rarely left. Gullit and Desailly were there in and around the same time, too.

Even without Zola, Ancelotti's men still took that season by storm as they finished second; only two points behind Juventus who, incidentally, failed to overcome Parma in either of their meetings that season. *Il Crociati* even beat them at home in January. There were some encouraging signs.

A number of formidable entries added to the growing index of the coach's earlier years in management. After assessing his squad, and with the Zola saga probably still ringing fresh in his ears, it appears Ancelotti's ways were set by 1997/98, in that he would seek out the necessary reinforcements best accustomed to the way he wanted to play – and do away with potential disruptors who might have to meet a similar fate to Zola if they failed to fall in line. This would mean having to miss out on natural creators for the sake of preserving the team's balance and the strength of his choices. Which would turn out to be a lesson on how inflexibility can cost you, once Roberto Baggio became available.

While on the subject of Baggio it is necessary to turn to nicknames. We call the great Ronaldo Nazario *O Fenômen, a* reflection of his phenomenal talent and storybook legacy. The equally great Edson Nascimento is called *'Pele*, either paying homage to a friend of his dad's who helped him train as a youngster at Santos, or a word that derived from his hometown in Bauru. Even he isn't sure. Then we have Roberto Baggio nicknamed the Divine Ponytail, to reflect his hairstyle and his Buddhist beliefs. Baggio was more than capable of standing out on talent alone, it must be said. A suave, sophisticated, ballet-like playmaker whose best years came during the genesis of the modern-day *trequartista*. Described by Sam Tigha for *Bleacher Report* as a role which requires 'superb ball skills, a good range of passing and confidence in possession', it frees up the designated stylist to do what they do best while relying on the strength of the men behind them to balance the scales. Tigha continues: 'defensive contribution is negligible, so someone plying their trade in this role can tailor their training specifically to take-ons, dribbling, through-balls and shooting' – a fitting playbook for the ever-inventive ponytailed maestro. Experienced broadcaster and journalist Carlo Garganese recalls in 2011 a time when Italian football hosted some of the best *trequartisti* around, and cites Zola and Baggio as exemplary figures. The pair were all about making an impression, getting fans into the seats and wowing them once they sat down. The Divine one once even said: 'I have never really been satisfied by the easily scored goal'. I believe him.

It's difficult to pinpoint when Baggio was at his best, as situations began to dictate how effective he was at his various clubs. Juventus and Capello's Milan spoiled their star with a plethora of defensive talent. By 1997, he had become disillusioned with the directionless Milan regime and looked for somewhere where he could once again be the main man. So, why not Parma? They had finished second in Serie A the previous season, they were clearly blessed with promising talent, a ready-made mix of domestic graduates and cultural imports, and the loving Parmese support to pick him up if he became down. For him, few places were as ideal and he reportedly did everything he could to make it happen. Even Parma's sporting director, Riccardo Sogliano, was a Baggio fan, and worked with the Milanese representatives to do some of the ground work on a potential transfer.

He could have moved on to most places in Europe – there were reports a move to England was on the cards – but Baggio was a homely man, and perhaps needed to make a trade from playing for an expectant 'big club' to trying out an underdog. I'm sure the fans would have wanted it, and the board was clearly keen on it too. But there was one man who was opposed … Carlo Ancelotti.

Sensing a repeat of the Zola situation and not wanting to house someone who would not adhere to his regimented tactical script, Ancelotti believed that his side needed another formation-fitting addition to the squad rather than a creative disruptor akin to Zola or Baggio. So, when Baggio became available Ancelotti barely batted an eyelid. He only engaged with the speculation when Baggio himself professed an interest in joining Parma. Ancelotti swatted away an army of paparazzi who couldn't make sense of his reason for ignoring one of Italy's most treasured players.

Ancelotti did sign a *Rossoneri* forward, but it was Jesper Blomqvist, whose form scaled from a disappointing game-by-game return in Milan, to a few less-than-disappointing spritely showings in a Parma shirt. As for Baggio, he moved to relative minnows Bologna – where he scored 22 goals that same season – propelling them to eighth, only two places below Ancelotti's men. Simple maths suggests that biting the Baggio bullet would have brought Parma much closer to champions Juventus, but things are never that simple in football. It was, however, a big regret for Ancelotti, but one from which he would learn.

> 'I said, "No, you have to play striker." Baggio went to another club. That year Baggio scored 25 [actually 22] goals – for Bologna! I lost 25 goals! Big mistake.'
>
> *Carlo Ancelotti on not signing Baggio in 1997/98 – Simon Kuper interview (*Financial Times, *2014)*

Understanding a need to wade into unfamiliar territory would come to be a steep learning curve for Ancelotti in the forthcoming season; when Juventus showed interest in plucking him from Parma.

Rivalry is a really funny thing in football so it's easy to see why many Juventus fans would have been reluctant to welcome Ancelotti to patrol their dugout. He was a fair candidate on merit, but it's tough to shake the kind of allegiance he had with their competitive rivals, Milan in particular.

They had been the two top dogs in Italy for as long as *calcio* has been around. Technically, their derby (if we can call it that) stands as the most repeated fixture of its type in the history of the Italian first division. Through this they have continually jostled back and forth for the right to be called the best club in the country.

Over the years, they've had to share everything; almost like brothers who want to be 'the better son'. The big stages, the big players, the bigger moments and international acclaim – it's exceedingly difficult to claim that one team is bigger than the other.

> 'At Juventus they hated me for playing at Milan, sometimes I had to be accompanied by the police.'
>
> *Carlo Ancelotti on his time as Juventus boss*

The Juventus fans even unfurled banners during his first game: 'A pig cannot coach' and 'Get out Ancelotti'. Ouch.

Common football irrationality aside, something that would help win over the fans would be to clear his act up when it came to his *trequartista* management. Because Juve had Zinedine Zidane, arguably the best all-round midfielder of his generation. Together, Juve only lost a single game across their first 26 in the league, with Ancelotti's midfield selection being almost alien from what he was using at Parma and Reggiana. Though he retained four at the back, this was the first sign of Ancelotti getting with the times and accommodating who he was given, rather than moulding them to fit his specifications. It was an apprenticeship in malleability and thinking on the spot upon orders from some of the most prestigious men in Italian football. For the first season, at least, this worked well, with Zidane proving pivotal to Juve's consistency in the league before they unexpectedly fell off towards the end of the season to finish second, a point adrift of Lazio.

Looking to get some momentum going for his second season, perhaps because Juve had scored only six goals in the final seven games the previous year, Ancelotti sought an additional striker. But even the acquisition of the enormously talented David Trezeguet from Monaco – who went on to become their top goalscorer in his first season in Turin – could not stop lightning striking twice. This time they were ahead of Lazio but now they were behind Roma.

Ancelotti was sacked before the season ended and, if the reports are to be believed, in pretty shameless circumstances. In an episode described by Tim Collins from *Bleacher Report* as 'almost inconceivable' if it wasn't true, Ancelotti was fired on the final day of the season during the final game at the half-time interval. Even more unbelievable, Juventus were not completely out of the title race when they told him. The two-point deficit to which they would ultimately succumb was the situation at the beginning of the day's fixtures.

Roma needed a win against a promising Parma side to remain top, while Juve needed to overcome Atalanta to keep up the pressure. Simple arithmetic reasons that a loss (or maybe even a draw) for Roma and a win for Juventus – both more than possible – would bring the trophy back to Turin.

Atalanta lasted only eight minutes before Alessandro Del Piero fired Juventus ahead, leading to a brief, ten-minute period of ecstasy before Francesco Totti drew first blood for Roma. By half-time, Roma had managed to double their lead, while Ancelotti's men stayed at 1-1 but looking equally good value for the win. Things weren't looking bright but at the time of the sacking Carlo Ancelotti was still within moments of winning the *Scudetto* title.

Throughout his career, both as player and manager, Ancelotti developed a reputation for being a sturdy, proud professional with a love of clarity, communication, ethics and positivity. This deserted him at Juventus. His term as Juve coach showed what can happen when you are not properly backed.

While improvising a reason to explain the inexplicable, the Juve president Umberto Agnelli reported to the press: 'The reason for Ancelotti's departure is that it is difficult to work in a city where the great part of the fans and the press are against you.' Trust Agnelli to blame the press – in front of the press – for his own decision.

But if we were to take that (and those aforementioned lack of assurances) at face value, it looks like Ancelotti was never properly suited to the Juventus post. It was a battle probably not likely to be won even with a *Scudetto* on the final day.

So, 800 days, 63 wins, 33 draws, 18 defeats, several disrespectful banners, an awkward president and Ancelotti was on the hunt once again.

Hopefully he'd find somewhere he'd feel wanted.

'Getting the Office Ready'

Coming into the 2000/01 season, AC Milan were what I would call 'a neutral's dream', a term often used by commentators to describe matches which, for fans of neither side, is action-packed, fraught with insecurity and had everything we'd want to see in a good game of football. So, imagine that happening, but in multiple matches throughout the year – matches in which the club looked as impressive as they were inconsistent.

That *Scudetto* trophy won under Zaccheroni in 1999 was basically all the *Rossoneri* had to write home about throughout this period of instability. But critically, the power of the Milan brand didn't subside. They were still more than capable of drawing in big names almost on prestige alone – ignoring who may actually be in charge, or if they would be fit for the job at hand. The direct predecessor to Ancelotti relied heavily on this. In fact, it might have been the main reason why he took up Berlusconi's offer in the first place.

Now we return to the enigmatic Turk Fatih Terim who joined the San Siro outfit after only a single year in charge of ninth-placed Fiorentina. There, he had managed big players and made some even bigger proclamations as to where he'd be able to take them if they followed his leadership to the letter. Ultimately, he failed, but outwardly claimed a difference of opinions with the business end of the Florence club as the main reason for why he couldn't break that mid-table threshold. Berlusconi called his bluff, and to his credit, he put that money of his to good use.

Without wanting to give everything away too prematurely, as we have a much bigger analysis coming up in the next couple of chapters, let's sign off by crediting Fatih Terim with – unwinnable gambles aside – buying some real game-changers for Milan in his short tenure, all of whom would benefit from his freeflowing tactical style during the few months he was in charge. They were to prove pivotal in the re-development of Milan under their next manager.

Following such a large collection of casualties, who believed that their ways were better than those preceding them, fate aligned for Milan to revert to type and end all the short-term nonsense. They finally welcomed back Carlo Ancelotti through a different door for a long-term project back at the San Siro.

He returned on 5 November 2001. A seasoned coach with a vendetta to settle.

> 'First of all, the fact that I went to coach Milan after playing there made it easier for me. I knew the club structures, some players … I felt really good because the support I had was really strong. I felt at home.'
>
> *Carlo Ancelotti on returning to Milan as manager in 2001.*

Before he could really settle his feet under the table and search for inspiration as to what to build next, there was the more immediate matter of getting the team back on course.

Under Terim, there's no skating around the fact that, while they were hugely entertaining to watch from an attacking front, their defensive issues were stopping them from reaching to where they wanted to be. Results may suggest that this is an overreaction, but watching footage from these games will reveal a starker reality. In my eyes, they were simply better at riding their luck and outsourcing their opponents whenever they got forward than controlling their fortune. This, mixed with the short-termism of a new manager and newer, exciting players led to a belief that it couldn't be sustained.

At his core, Terim was a personable, eccentric, hard-working manager who had probably wormed his way into Milanese hearts around the world. On top of what we saw earlier, Paolo Maldini even did his best to stand strong against the tide when Terim was threatened with the sack: explaining that any insufficiencies on the manager's part 'was also our failure'. Even the club's ultimate decision-makers 'thought again and again' about the best avenue to take moving forward, before a dismissal appeared 'the best decision to take'. But in a statement issued to the press when their new manager was selected, they insisted: 'A new chapter has begun. Ancelotti returns to his Milan, where he was a key player.' And that, from this point on, 'it will be a new team'.

In order to be successful, Ancelotti understood that he needed to address this blocker element – by all means, win matches, but make sure the team understand the importance of both defending their position and entertaining those needy spenders on the terraces.

I'm keen to reject the notion that Ancelotti was a 'defensive manager'. How can you win as much as he did by defending all the time? Though reports from the time suggest Berlusconi wasn't too happy with his manager's apparently negative disposition when it came to setting up his teams. Fortunately, a fourth-placed finish in this first season (and just-about Champions League qualification) was good enough. It was also a good starting point from which to attack the forthcoming season. He'd also have a full transfer window to work with.

CHAPTER FIVE

'Laying the Foundations'

BY HIS own standards, Ancelotti shelled out some Fatihesque bucks of his own, but he did it in a characteristically measured way. Noticing that Milan's biggest problems lay in defence, he sought to address the gaps at the back before thinking ahead of the halfway line.

The man Ancelotti turned to in trying to shore up this weakness was Alessandro Nesta, the centrepiece of the Lazio team that had won the *Scudetto* in 2000 and he had been Serie A Defender of the Year three times in a row.

Nesta had shown signs of competence during his early Lazio days, even if it took a lengthy positional experiment to get him there. Under the watchful eyes of the *Laziali* staff, he was allowed to discover which area of the pitch was best suited to his talent.

He wasn't as quick, nimble or tricky as some of the wing-players, so venturing wide was never his destiny. The spine of the team was far more suitable. He was tried in central midfield, even at striker – before Dino Zoff chose him as a centre-back. And that's where he stayed to develop further under the instruction of new manager Zdeněk Zeman.

> 'In Italy, managers are afraid that losing a game might mean losing their job. That's why most teams ... tend to not make the opponents play, rather than play themselves. You have to make every effort ... in order not to lose. That's miles away from my mentality.'
>
> *An insight into Zeman's football theory*

Zeman's view was that football was wasted on preserving a lead for pride's sake. To him, going 1-0 up served merely as a buffer to go even further and show your strength. It directly contravened the pragmatism of the era, and was rarely conducive to long-term success, but it was liberating for learners like Nesta.

Nesta wasn't confined to a set of principles that might end up defining him; instead his formative experience encouraged him to explore the breadth of his ability. Since working with him, Nesta labels Zeman as a 'misunderstood genius [who] played a fundamental role in [his] career'. Sure, his views were polarising, but there was a microcosmic method to the macrocosmic madness. Some Italian fans even had a name for it: 'Zemanlandia'. Zeman encouraged younger players to explore their qualities and see what they liked best, rather than cramming a square peg into a round hole and hoping for the best. 'There are many coaches today who only manage, without trying to improve their players,' Zeman said. 'Then there are a few coaches who shape players. I feel like one of these few.' Most of the Italian football community would be inclined to agree, I'm sure.

By the turn of the millennium, Nesta developed into a key feature for Lazio, captaining a star-studded line-up to a league and Coppa Italia double in 2000.

Players like Pavel Nedvěd, Juan Sebastian Verón and Christian Vieri linked up to devastating effect for the *Laziali* before financial disaster befell then-president Sergio Cragnotti, a man who, though generally reviewed as an aloof leader loosely guided by emotion over sense, was a focal point in some of Lazio's most noteworthy chapters, even if that meant opening his own fiscal position to scrutiny if things didn't go his way. Unfortunately, that's exactly what happened.

He rested on his food business empire as a means for financing Lazio's nouveau riche ambitions, and the foundations of this rocked as the strains of the club required more active involvement from Cragnotti's reserves. Cirio, a tinned tomato company (and a key part to the bank account) was even the sponsor of Lazio's kit at one point, showing how essential the two were as they sought to shore up Lazio.

Cirio was unable to sustain the pressure and eventually they caved. Funds were frozen, players went unpaid and Lazio's best players (hereby known as 'assets') were seized. Not by banks but by greedy, opportunistic vultures who could do what their employers couldn't. Soon enough, Nesta, Nedvěd, Verón and pretty much everybody else was on a flight away from Rome. For the club it was a disastrous fall from the heights they thought they had reached when winning the *Scudetto*.

Depressingly, Nesta reflects that he had even rejected advances from Real Madrid only a season or two before Milan signalled their interest, and the way he waved them away shows how committed he was to the Lazio cause.

Such are the wonders of modern technology that he confessed much of his feelings about this experience during an Instagram Live session with Christian Vieri. 'At the time, I didn't want to go anywhere – I would have stayed there for life.' Pretty committed, if you ask me. But 'it was hard because the locker room was a mess. I was the captain and I was part of the board of directors. I was 23 and they were talking about the club's balance, it was very stressful.' Altogether, a chance to re-focus on what he does best was a welcome tonic for him in this next stage of his career. But that didn't mean it wouldn't hurt.

Despite his clear quality and professionalism, I can imagine it was a little bit tougher of an embedding process than history cares to remember for Nesta at Milan.

Whatever preconception we may have of football players and the apparent easiness of their lifestyle, they are human too. Subject to human frailties and driven by human motivations. Alessandro Nesta wanted to be a football player because he loved the game of football. He wanted to represent Lazio because he was a fan – as was his father. So, you can imagine draping on that sky blue jersey wasn't about simply representing an employer and picking up a pay cheque by the time he took it off. It was about emulating the players he grew up watching, and lying in his bed every night satisfied with the idea that he was now that figure for other future players.

Moving to Milan would also relieve Nesta of the captain's armband, which he'd worked so tirelessly to earn. It was a potential problem for the club and the player if the situation wasn't managed properly.

From Milan's view, at the least, they were securing a well-respected member of a high-profile club who would arrive readily accustomed to the stresses of the top-flight lifestyle. Ideally, this might help to elevate the overall performance of new team members. On the flip side, there might be an ego problem. Players who go from being the 'go-to man' around a campus, might struggle to adjust to a dressing room full of similarly big personalities. Thankfully, it was Nesta and Ancelotti, a consummate professional and man-manager duo capable of voicing and addressing issues before they got out of hand.

Fittingly, Nesta featured in just shy of 50 matches in his first season with Milan, with any tangible criticism dissipating after his first two or three. They scored 17 times in their first five games, conceding only two. One of those was against Lazio, but with typical Ancelotti conscientiousness (and good timing), he didn't even play the whole game. Thumping Torino 6-0 in the next fixture ideally stifled any awkwardness that followed.

For the remainder of the season, various partners were trialled alongside him. Kakhaber 'Kakha' Kaladze, Martin Laursen, even a time-battling Alessandro Costacurta, but that lack of security proved fatal at domestic level. Milan fell 11 points short of Juventus, and ultimately finished third; behind Inter too! But it was a stand-out season for the suave centre-back.

On his own, Nesta went against the convention of being a typical defender with his naturally offensive mindset. Positionally, he would still hold his station for large portions of the game, then his mental wherewithal kicked into gear once the waters had calmed, and the ball fell under his spell. I can't think of too many 'modern' defenders who possess Nesta's technique. He was, quite literally, a striker told to play in defence. But even strikers need a solid, effective partnership in a formation like this to be successful in the long term.

A year watching what Nesta was capable of revealed the gap to be plugged. To complement Nesta's grace and elegance, strength and solidity was needed. Which, ironically, took Ancelotti back to Lazio.

First in 2003, Giuseppe Pancaro arrived in a direct exchange deal which saw Demetrio Albertini go in the opposite direction. Albertini's technical ability was beyond sound, especially when it came to running with the ball at pace and carrying it between the lines. He did this on multiple occasions and formed an efficient cog in the Milanese machine during his most effective period in a *Rossoneri* shirt.

Pancaro – though stationed a little further back – was a good replacement, in mind and matter. He had played with Nesta in Lazio's glory days and the two picked up where they left off in red and black. Pancaro was a workhorse, and had few airs or graces about having to muddy his boots and crunch into his opponent while Nesta did all the fancy stuff. Most great defensive partnerships are made using a similar recipe. If things had panned out differently, history would remember Pancaro and Nesta as another of Milan's great central partnerships. But Pancaro was 33 years old by the 2003/04 season, aged further by his combative lifestyle no doubt. Mentally, he probably could have lasted a little longer, but pragmatically the most sensible thing would have been to search for a defender like him with a later use-by date.

Luckily for Ancelotti and Milan, Lazio had another player, similar to him if not a teency-weensy bit more intense. Enter Dutchman Jaap Stam.

'I loved the physical nature of the game in England, but in Serie A I only have to look at a player and they sometimes fall to the floor!'

- Jaap Stam

Intimidation formed a major part of Jaap Stam's MO, but that should not distract from his innate ability as a danger-sensing defender. Because of his size, he was not agile or quick but he had a steely determination to win and a broad frame.

When reading Peter Schmeichel's autobiography *ONE*, it became clear that players like he and Jaap were hard-wired to tap into their wild side. When, in a *Terminator*-like fashion, their brain locked on to a goal the rest of their body fell in line. When you're built like this, sometimes impulses take over. You go for that 50-50, when really it's a 70-30. You kid the medical staff that you're feeling much better than you are because otherwise you can't play. You basically put the needs of the team ahead of your own, even if it takes a toll on you in the long run. It's things like these which get the fans on your side and is a good, non-verbal way of elevating the performance of those around you. 'I understood at that moment that to have the starting position, I had to work my ass off every day.'

Stam wasn't just a battering ram bereft of technique and over-reliant on physicality. He was a physical defender but it was generally both fit for his purpose and for the era in which he played. His invasion of a striker's privacy was measured and calculated. His aim was to get the ball, not the player. But if the player got in his way and succumbed to his power that was their problem, not his.

Stam's reading of the game should also be commended, because while he wasn't the quickest he was rarely caught out. His aggression was of value to him. All good defensive players are combative in nature – they aren't afraid of getting into a scrap with their opposite number, even if it means putting their body at risk, as explained by the late Jack Charlton: 'you can't play the game of football without having a little bit of aggression', theorising that, in order to retrieve possession from the opponent, you need that bit of anger to 'know that you're going to get it, and it's going to be yours'. Match this with Stam's technical qualities and you have a defender who seldom attracted unwanted attention, and was wanted by some of the best clubs in the world.

Before coming to Italy, Stam's name was put in the spotlight by shining performances for PSV Eindhoven and the Netherlands national team before his club welcomed the advances of the then-globe-conquering Manchester United. He joined them in 1998 for a fee believed to be around £14 million – a princely sum for a central defender back then. But nevertheless a worthy one.

Three trophy-laden seasons came and went in England before controversy struck in 2001. It led to one of the most infamous sales in United's modern history. Throughout his career their manager Sir Alex Ferguson had an enormous amount of success, difficult to sustain without making the occasional mistake. Selling Stam, as he begrudgingly admitted, fell into that category.

'It was one of the mistakes I made –
hopefully I haven't made too many – but
that was one.'

Sir Alex Ferguson

At the time, the *Guardian* reported the 'shock'
move as one that was an enormous gamble for a
transitioning Manchester United. But while they
went on what turned out to be a long voyage to
stabilise a leaky defence without Stam, Lazio
were the beneficiaries, whisking him away for
£16-or-so million. At the same time they were also
employing Nesta.

Another controversy would deny us the
pleasure of watching Jaap and Nesta play a full-
strength season in Lazio colours. Firstly because
Nesta was sold in 2002, secondly because Stam
was banned from playing for a month after testing
positive for the banned substance nandrolone by
Italy's National Olympic Committee. It was a bit
of a farce.

Proclaiming his innocence, Stam still
vehemently denies any claim of having knowingly
taken the substance in a bid to improve his football
performance. I'm inclined to believe him for two

reasons: his own account and common footballing sense. Regarding the first, Stam was not the only high-profile player to fall foul of the NOC; in fact, he was not the only Dutch player involved. Both Edgar Davids and Frank De Boer – from the same international camp, of course – were found to have traces of nandrolone in their systems. All three sought medical advice about the food supplements they were having, and possessed proof of their diet. Stam spoke out at the time about the character of his team-mates, and maintains that he would have stood up in a courtroom on their behalf had he been asked.

Secondly, the idea that players as mature as Stam, Davids and De Boer were stupid and insecure enough to put their careers at risk is beyond me. Thankfully, the Italian authorities agreed, reducing Stam's original five-month suspension to just a month.

With hindsight, it's easy to think that a single month's suspension for a bogus claim would not have affected a year which still had about 90 per cent left to play. But you still have a high-profile signing who's been suspended before he could even get there. It was awkward, perpetuated by some poor decisions at a higher level that deprived us of a top Lazio season for Stam and his new team-mates.

Fate would intervene three years later when Stam and Nesta fell foul of Lazio's boardroom drama. And by the time a 32-year-old Jaap Stam grew tired of the issues in Rome, Nesta, now embedded at the San Siro, was ready to welcome him with open arms.

Although Stam is only an inch taller than Nesta, it's still astounding to note the difference of stature between the two. Imagine you're a striker and you confront the duo. You have Nesta, suave and devilishly handsome, who appears to have misplaced his three-piece Armani suit in the dressing room. Then you have Stam, who looks like he only wears a suit for occasions requiring a phone, an assassin and an order to be made. Very different, very conflicting.

They'd probably cross the finishing line at the same time in a 100m race, but they were a symphony of balance in the heart of that Milan defence. That same season, Ancelotti wasted little time in making sure that the chemistry between the two was as good as it could possibly be. Instead of having to manage other top central defenders most of Stam's would-be competitors went out of the same door through which he came. Roque Júnior? Martin Laursen? Fabricio Coloccini? All gone.

It left Stam and Nesta to bear the burden of Milan's most critical games throughout a season when they finished second in the league, lifted the Supercoppa Italiana and the Champions League.

But just in case some daring fellow managed to jink their way past these two, Ancelotti needed a last-minute lock on the door and for this he chose Dida. Standing at 6ft 4in tall, with arms almost as long as his legs, Dida fitted the coach's requirements to a tee.

> 'Living in Milan and playing for AC Milan, with the fans that we have here and all over the world, it is very special.'
>
> *Dida*

Dida was among the very few whose size belied his speed. He was quick. He was agile. He was also confident. And it's that final element of his character which elevated him to the heights he achieved in Milan. There's nothing more detrimental to your squad than an unconfident goalkeeper. It is critical that a goalkeeper is cool-tempered and displays an aura which says to the opposition 'you aren't going to beat me', because this feeds through into the squad much more than a striker who's off their game, or a creator who's blind for a few matches. Temperament lends itself to consistency, too. A series of experiments conducted in a study titled *Theory and Practice of Physical Culture* revealed that goalkeepers tend to be more prone to stubbornness and frustration than their team-mates, but score lower in the ego charts. The inference is that their motivation is team focused.

Suppose you make a brilliant save as a goalkeeper; a striker caresses the ball tenderly, it looks destined for the corner of the net, then you reach it at full stretch to tip it for a corner kick. But any celebrations are short-lived. The danger hasn't gone. After all those heroics, you have to put aside euphoria, tell the adrenaline to quieten down and get ready to defuse another potential threat. You wouldn't even get the time to steady yourself for a set piece if your save ricochets back into play – then you've got to improvise.

Then, in situations where nothing's imminent you've got to command your area, organise your defence, arrange your walls and still escape most fair lauds from pundits who refuse to comment on a goalkeeper until they make a mistake. The mental strength and acuity required to work through something like this isn't to be sniffed at. Dida would develop it over time. While Dida ticked a lot of the obvious 'good goalkeeper' boxes – physical stature, confidence in the air, bravery in the 50-50s, broad vocality, decent distribution technique, and a good pair of hands in one-on-ones – he had to work hard for the privilege of being Milan's number one.

Unlike many of his compatriots who found their way to Europe through their distinction at club level from Brazil, Dida's fame came from the international scene. Which took a fortuitous turn in 1995.

That year, revered *Seleção* pick and regular starter, Claudio Taffarel sustained a niggle in the run up to the *Copa America*, so Dida was drafted. But instead of assuming that role of the understudy who reminds the audience of where they are in relation to the first choice, Dida played a key role in sustaining his country's challenge for the title until Taffarel returned. Brazil eventually lost to Uruguay 5-3 on penalties after a 1-1 scoreline at full time, but it was an invaluable learning experience for the inexperienced stopper. The Olympics in Atlanta followed in 1996 and Dida was no. 1 for what was basically an under-23 team.

He recovered well after an early setback in Brazil's opener to Japan, before eventually succumbing to a Kanu 'golden goal' in extra time against Nigeria to leave with the bronze medal. The 1998 World Cup was more a test of character for Dida than anything constructive. He had fallen to third in the goalkeeping pecking order and struggled to feature in Brazil's controversial campaign in France. It left the 25-year-old with a crucial decision to make.

He could either stick it out in Brazil, maybe getting a promotion to a more prestigious club side or he could continue his evolution elsewhere in the belief that better coaching facilities and higher quality opposition would tell him if he was truly cut out for life as a top-drawer goalkeeper. Bravely, he opted for the latter. Again, it wouldn't be easy.

Few suitors lined up to take the Brazilian on an immediate, first-team deal. It has been suggested that a couple of lesser-known La Liga sides were 'keeping tabs on him' but it was Milan who proposed the most sensible and concrete offer for him. Tabling an offer north of £2 million with a plan to loan him back to perennial table-toppers, Corinthians, it was a deal which suggested 'just in case' even if it was not explicitly stated in those terms.

This kind of arrangement is a form of insurance for the bidder. For Milan, it was a no-brainer. Pay a couple of million, test him out in higher waters, and probably make their money back if they need to sell him. Corinthians would get an established local goalkeeper on their books, with an added impression that he's worthy of a club like Milan. However, for Dida, it was make or break. Impress or it's done.

This time, it was a different story. Not only did he do well at Corinthians, but his intended two-year loan spell was cut short when Milan required competition for an ageing Sebastiano Rossi, and the internationally involved Christian Abbiati. After a few stutters along the way – including some sort of issue with his passport which the Italian Football Federation flagged in 2002 – he joined the *Rossoneri* full-time for the 2002/03 season. An injury to Abbiati allowed Dida to finish the remainder of a key UEFA Champions League qualifier against FC Slovan Liberec. Milan won the game, Dida kept a clean sheet and Ancelotti had little choice but to promote him to a starting spot.

Most might have caved under the expectations of the Milan jersey – especially in the company of the defence they had at the time – but Dida was impressive in his first season for *I Diavolo*, with his bravery and communication skills largely to thank for pacifying those early doubters. And as he grew into his role, it freed some space in Ancelotti's mind to address the team's flashier areas; knowing that his last line of defence would only solidify as time drifted by.

CHAPTER SIX

'Drawing the Blueprint'

ADHERING TO Berlusconi's unofficial, yet clear 'I want a fluid and interesting four at the back, or else you'll end up like Zaccheroni' warning, Ancelotti could rest easy knowing that one defensive berth was sorted at least for the near future.

The evolution of a certain Paolo Maldini came full circle to calm his manager's insecurities about the left-back position.

Testament to his stratospheric career, even Maldini's debut is a talking point – as a substitute for the injured Sergio Battistini in Serie A against Udinese, a side housed in the historical city of Udine and host to a talisman by the name of Arthur Antunes Coimbra, better recognised by his nickname 'Zico'. Yes, The Zico. But the inexperienced Maldini refused to be caught unawares by the mastery of the Brazilian. It was a feature telling enough for Paolo to earn the odd involvement in his debut campaign in 1985 under Liedholm, who was quick to recognise the need to develop his precocious utility man. He even handed him the number 3 shirt from the off, a shirt previously worn by his father, Cesare. With the Swede's hand on his shoulder, Maldini would struggle to figure out which area of the pitch he enjoyed most, but with his careful pre-match preparation and outstanding application for long-term play, there'd be more than enough time. He would develop a myriad of techniques from the managers who came and went, before becoming a key figure on the left side. There, he rested quietly like a wizard watching on as the team changed before him. Maldini's stature even led to an approach from Alex Ferguson at Old Trafford, but when confronted with the broad, unassuming frame of his proud Milanese father, it was clear that there was no manoeuvrability on his stance. 'He was quite formidable,' Fergie admits. 'I got a shake of the head' was his final remark. Cesare himself declared his family's oath to Milan. 'My grandfather was Milan, my father's Milan, I'm Milan, my sons are Milan.'

In this social media world of capturing every moment and sharing it with whoever will engage, I rest easy knowing that 'Paolo Maldini' would be a name on the lips of every football lover in the land. The grace with which he took the ball in his stride, his enviable knack of knowing where to be placed and at what time. He was as close to football perfection as it is possible to conceive. If you think that's a grandiose statement, you'd be right.

As we know, Maldini was a critical brick in the 'invincible' wall under Capello on the left of a back four. Then, when Franco and Mauro eventually left the club in 1996/97, and the team needed a captain, Paolo was the logical successor. I imagine that meant a great deal to the lifelong *Rossonero* – and he refused to let anyone else wear the armband full-time until his own retirement in 2009. The resulting parade to bid farewell to their long-term leader was a 'wonderful surprise' for a man who might never truly realise how loved he was. And to spend such a long period of this success as captain for his favourite club was 'one of the most satisfying experiences I have ever had', he said through tears to a *New York Post* reporter shortly after his party. To put this enormous achievement into some sort of perspective, most top players wouldn't get an opportunity to play a decade at the fiercer end of European competition. Maldini captained one of Europe's best ever teams for longer than that. In all he played 902 games for Milan, and is not surprisingly top of their appearances list. Second-placed Franco Baresi made 716 appearances.

Ancelotti was smart enough to leave the team leadership structure untouched, and drafting in the likes of Stam and Nesta enabled his captain to stay where he was most comfortable, instead of having to fill in at centre-back like he did on occasion when one or the other was missing. Fierce Georgian Kakha Kaladze would do his best to make up for either of their omissions across the middle when needed, and usually did so well enough for the other not to be missed for too long. Kaladze was a tough, not-to-mess-with presence much as Stam was.

Of the existing players capable of playing on the right side of defence, Alessandro Costacurta and Giuseppe Pancaro now had a combined age of just over 70 and they needed someone with flair, physical strength, pace, a forward-thinking brain and a mentality for knuckling down and doing things properly. A sprinkle of demonstrable experience at the top level wouldn't go amiss either.

Remarkably, he found his man. And didn't even have to pay for him.

> 'People tend to forget that defensively he was very strong, but he stands out because of his attacking impulses and energy. Cafu just kept going – up and down, up and down – and never gave up.'
>
> *Jaap Stam*

In recent times, the received wisdom appertaining to the right-back position (or full-backs in general) has become distorted. Traditionalists tend to adopt a 'defending comes first' mentality, in which attacking qualities come second to their ability to stop opponents from doing the same thing.

Modernists think the opposite: reasoning that the slicker, quicker surfaces of today call out for technicians on the flanks to make the most of what's in front of them. I consider myself leaning 65 per cent towards tradition. I want solidity from my right-back. Where they stop what they need to stop, and don't neglect that duty because they're caught too far forward. But I also want them to, when the situation calls for it, have enough intelligence and ability to take the ball at their feet and see what their creativity suggests they do next. The best teams tend to have a nice blend of both options in their full-back regions. Take the Brazilian national team as an example:

In 1970 they had Carlos Alberto, a very gifted right-back, forever immortalised for his unconventional, yet telepathic understanding with Pelé. Together, their work morphed into some of the most expansive, revolutionary examples of what would become normal in the world of football. Alberto demonstrated a level of intelligence and maturity to know which part of that spectrum to focus on and when.

Fast forward three-to-four decades, and Dani Alves became the most decorated footballer in history; normalising and improving upon the very principles practised by Alberto. He earned accolades aplenty for various clubs with a similarly well-rounded technical arsenal. Sandwiched between the pair of them, Cafu was Brazil's representative for the 90s and 00s.

Having developed into a raw, yet full of character wing-back under the guidance of Telê Santana in São Paulo and Luiz Felipe Scolari in a star-producing Palmeiras side in the mid-90s, he would blossom fully at AS Roma under Zdeněk Zeman, who as he had done with Alessandro Nesta, refined Cafu's own wayward habits.

Naturally, Cafu was an exuberant South American who wanted to get involved in the attack wherever possible. But with the manager's words in his ear, he slowly learned that an all-out, gung-ho style might not be advisable all of the time. Zeman liked a high defensive line, which is why a lot of his teams were so fun to watch.

But to make sure his side didn't concede every time they were attacked, his defence had to be impeccably placed so as to not be easily caught out on the counter, especially the full-backs in relation to their respective central defender.

When quizzed on the subject of Zeman's defensive teachings – or lack thereof – Cafu smiled: 'We did do some defensive drills, but tactically they were shocking; our offside trap was set almost in the middle of the pitch. It was suicide! Zeman didn't care and wanted us to play like that in league matches.'

Altogether, Cafu spent six seasons in the Italian capital, running his way into every Roman heart in the process under the name *Il Pendolino*, which, depending on the dialect, can mean 'The Commuter' or 'The Express Train'. My British mind finds an insult in the former, whereas the latter sounds cooler, so let's stick with that. Anyway, once Mr Train's contract was up in 2003, few begrudged from seeking pastures new. Especially as his prime years seemed to be behind him.

He was 33 years old at this point, and it was largely expected that he was going to settle down with a few less strenuous years en route to retirement, ideally in a less competitive league on a short-term deal with favourable contract terms. J-League club Yokohama Marinos looked as though they'd won the race. Cafu signed a pre-contract with them in the winter period of the previous season – promising to link with his new team-mates for the start of the next. The then Yokohama president, Shigeo Hidaritomo, claimed the formalities 'had been sorted out' and didn't feel the need to hide his pride when asked about his new signing. 'We are really proud about Cafu's signing,' he gushed, 'because we know that we will bring one of the best players in the world to Japan ... with him in our side, we can win domestic and continental trophies.'

So, a two-and-a-half-year deal (reportedly worth $3.5 million), an adoring set of executives ready to market you as their 'main man', the opportunity to explore a new culture and settle down into post-playing serenity. What could possibly go wrong?

It seems it was claimed that the SARS epidemic was a significant stumbling block to the deal. Though logic – and Cafu's story – suggests that an opportunity to join AC Milan was too good to turn down. When he was approached by Milan, only 15 days before he was supposed to be presented at Yokohama, Cafu remembers calling the Yokohama officials to explain his side of the story and promptly reimbursed them for the fees they'd wired over to sweeten his deal. I can't begin to imagine how awkward that call must have been, but his reason was simple: 'I wouldn't have been able to live with myself if I'd refused a club like Milan.'

The general consensus was that, though he was a remarkable player, he'd struggle to commit to more than a few half-seasons as age caught up with him. But *Il Pendolino* had some Maldini-esque age-defying tricks up his own sleeve. He became a key player in the back line alongside his new team-mates, and with his acquisition, the defence was practically complete.

I'm going to go out on a limb here and say that this defence – similar to pretty much the rest of the first team – was the best of its time. They might not have achieved quite the feats that others did in this period, but if we were to highlight the specific qualities of the players, and how they balanced each other on the pitch, they really were second to none.

> 'We have the best defence in the world, [but] we are a team that is designed to attack and think more about scoring than defending.'
>
> *Carlo Ancelotti* (c.2004)

On that note, if we agree that modern opinions are split on what is expected from a full-back, we see a fairly united front when it comes to explaining the importance of the defensive midfielder. It is now a common narrative that you won't be able to achieve anything of real note without having that counterbalance in the midfield, a go-between to take the side seamlessly from defence through to attack.

Over time, some of the best examples have treated this position in their own idiosyncratic way, almost to the point where their version creates an eponymous edition of the role, an example from which future generations can draw inspiration. I've already mentioned a couple.

The effervescent, ever-ready Falcão, a man hell-bent on disturbing the formation he faced with the view of carving out an opportunity for his side; the immortal-come-invincible Frank Rijkaard who was never afraid to put his limbs where it hurt if the ball was in reach. They were about as different in style as they looked in appearance, but effective nonetheless.

Truth be told, the role has evolved to a point where it now escapes a certain 'type'. Some see themselves as the introduction to the defence, others an entry way into the attack. Some like to be combative, visceral – others prefer the fancy game. For every Graeme Souness, there's a Johan Neeskens. With every Roy Keane, comes a Lothar Matthäus. The position is whatever its appointee decrees it to be. But critically, the mould is formed and distorted to a point where it serves a purpose depending on the solidity and/or fragility of the rest of the team.

As I hope I've been able to communicate, Milan were far from fragile. They were tough and confident, which was exactly what they needed from their pivot.

Gennaro Gattuso's route to the big time wasn't not conventional. His story exudes the sense of a man who aims to clasp on to the fortunes life has provided for him. For he knows how perilous that position is.

Run-of-the-mill stints with lesser-known Serie A sides appear on Gattuso's résumé as they tend to for the majority of his compatriots. Perugia and Salernitana are the names we would read on his. Sandwiched between them, however, was one of my favourite coming-of-age decisions I've seen, especially in the modern era. Following a decent few seasons breaking through into the Perugia first team, it could have been very easy, and largely expected, for the Italian midfielder to eke out a career in other similar settings. Perhaps a couple of solid campaigns in top-flight Italian football might gain the attention of the national team. Then, maybe he could find himself atop the wish-list of one of the bigger domestic clubs. Then, double maybe, he could venture into the unknown in a foreign league. There was another way, however. All he had to do was pretty much reverse the process and hope for the best.

Make no mistake, moving abroad at a young age, in any vocation, not just football, takes a heap of mental strength. Not only could it derail your career if you prove over-reliant on home comforts, but all of those external adjustments could ruin the natural order of where you want your career to end up. Realistically, only the best can really get through it unscathed. Jude Bellingham, Jadon Sancho, Erling Haaland – basically anybody Dortmund fancy – are good examples.

They all could have easily remained in the comfort zone where they grew up but that wasn't enough for them. They sought a journey that, while harder, would reap greater rewards if they were good enough to overcome the hurdles.

All that mattered was their desire to take hold of their career and pilot a success of their own making. Gennaro Gattuso had an opportunity to understand exactly what that would feel like in 1997. Certain stand-out performances in an international youth tournament caught the attention of many a glinting eye. Among them were the formidably experienced pupils of Rangers manager, Walter Smith.

'When I played for Perugia, deep down I thought I lacked the mental strength to go out on the pitch and play without the fear of making a mistake. But when I arrived in Scotland, everything was completely different. Glasgow was the place where I first started to think like a professional footballer.'

Gattuso on leaving Italy in 1997

Smith always struck me as somebody who is usually very sure of his assumptions, and his decision to offer Gattuso a four-year deal helps to develop that image. Based on little else than an exciting sprint with the Italian youth team and a few needs-must appearances in a Perugia shirt, there he was, see-sawing the attacking tendencies of Paul Gascoigne, Brian Laudrup and Ally McCoist. Adding a small bit of method to this madness, Walter Smith made sure his new young recruit was not lonely. He also signed Lorenzo Amoruso from Fiorentina, who did quite well, it must be said, Sergio Porrini from Juventus and Marco Negri – someone Gattuso was already well acquainted with from Perugia. I doubt Gattuso needed his friends close by to give him the confidence to express himself in Glasgow, as senior members of the Rangers camp would come to realise when they dared to dally with the ball anywhere near Gattuso in training.

Team-mates remember a fearlessness emanating from the Italian whenever he was in reach of dispossessing one of them. On that note, a likely apocryphal story exists where Gascoigne, loosely tasked as an impromptu translator for him (presuming he spent some time studying the local dialect during his time at Lazio), paraphrased his manager's instructions by encouraging Gattuso's enthusiasm rather than stifling it. Regardless of how the true account is, Gascoigne was still instrumental in helping Gattuso settle into his new home.

A better-proven story reads of the two taking regular trips into town to kit out the Italian in suits to wear on matchdays. Unaccustomed to the demands of playing for such a prestigious club, it should come as little surprise that a freshly pressed three-piece suit was not a feature of Gennaro's wardrobe. The pair went into town to right that wrong, where perhaps a lack of knowledge of the local exchange rate explained the £10,000 bill that needed settling. Gazza had apparently let on that the club held a partnership with this particular shop – freeing Gattuso of any inhibition to spend as little as possible. The truth proved that to be a white lie on Gazza's part, and he footed the bill himself for the cost of seeing his new team-mate with his guard down. Another heart-warming addition to the enigmatic personality that is Paul Gascoigne.

Suited, booted and firmly rooted in the art of being a Rangers player, the infamous Old Firm derby presented the ideal opportunity for Gennaro Gattuso to prove his worth.

While competitive rivalries between two big clubs are far from rare, the visceral hatred between Rangers and Celtic sets their meetings apart from the majority of local clashes in the game. Theirs grew from a seedling which supersedes football, and the feeling only seems to increase with every passing game. Now, it's reached the point where the Scottish authorities refuse to mix the fans on matchday. Apparently, that is a safety precaution, but it sucks out some of the atmosphere they used to have. This is why I click on to archives of older matches from time to time. The players, the personalities, the sounds, the grainy footage, the commentary, the fighting ... it's all a part of the experience. Many players would wilt under that volume of pressure, but not Gattuso.

Spending only one full season at the club, he had only two opportunities to appreciate Old Firm matches. But they proved an education of how to combine his ferocious mental acuity with his subtle ball-playing qualities, fostered during a purple patch of form for the Rangers brigade under a manager all too encouraging of exploring both sides of his footballing psyche. Apparently, there was a match when Gattuso sustained a cut over his eye and asked to come off for the second half. Smith requested stitches and Gattuso acquiesced.

Gattuso achieved greater things than he did during his single Scottish season, but it's good that he maintains an appreciation for his time there. In casting an eye back to Ibrox, Gattuso says: 'They taught me to combine aggression with loyalty. I am not the star player; I am more of a team player who gives every ounce of energy to the team. That was something instilled in me by Walter Smith at Rangers.'

It was losing Gascoigne to a derisory offer from Middlesbrough in March 1998 that signalled the beginning of the end for Gattuso. With Dick Advocaat's arrival Gattuso found himself back in Italy with Salernitana for the new season.

His year with Salernitana was good but most likely left the mercurial Italian with a burning desire to recapture some of the passion that had invigorated him at Rangers. Salernitana's own slapdash approach to financial management couldn't have helped either and the club even had to file for bankruptcy in 2005. But at least buying and selling Gattuso represented a rare 100 per cent profit when they sold him to Milan in 1999. Whereupon he would simultaneously lower the average age of the *Rossoneri* midfield, and enjoy a permanence within a setting that would cherish, rely on and respect his tenacious streak. Almost immediately, he exhibited the type of nastiness and uncompromising nature that wormed its way into the hearts of the Scots.

It was not until his second season at the San Siro that his name would be etched into Milan's history. It came in tandem with the paradoxical creativity of Andrea Pirlo.

CHAPTER SEVEN

'Getting the Decorators in'

ANDREA PIRLO is as suave as the day is long. I could watch him for as long as my eyelids would allow.

Unlike some of his team-mates, Pirlo was never really the athletic type. Don't get me wrong, a player must unequivocally dedicate himself to the physical side of the game to gain entry into its elite community. But it didn't really define Pirlo. Barring the odd need to over-extend his leg to pull the ball back under his spell, the majesty came from his unerringly effortless control over it.

Among many other things, creative midfielders are revered for their manipulation of a football.

'His vision, what he can do with the ball, and what he's able to create, make him a true superstar. Andrea has something which you don't see very often.'

Roberto Baggio

Pirlo's talent was a real exception to the norm, though it took a series of pivotal, conscious developments before he could enjoy the eventual fanfare that would follow his name.

Historically, AC Milan has maintained a tough, territorial relationship with the Lombardia region despite the city being its capital. Perhaps most famously, Franco Baresi was born in the region and tried out for a number of local clubs before being deemed not good enough and scouted by a Milan official. The stories of Costacurta and Albertini have similar origins, though Pirlo would be among the few to have actually represented a professional outfit from Lombardia before taking a 50-mile drive upstate. His journey began with Brescia Calcio, where he appeared the antithesis of the legend he'd eventually become.

We've grown accustomed to that debonair, confident swagger of a deep-lying playmaker who knows the game cannot continue without him. But as a youngster coming through at Brescia, even the classy Pirlo was not immune to the frivolities of youth. Running about the pitch with little consideration as to his impact, Pirlo found most of his involvement derived from an advanced forward position. Where, contrary to most technical attacking midfielders, he could be seen getting drawn into the attack more than for his own good at that time. Then manager Mircea Lucescu had a bit of a Zemanlandia approach to things, and welcomed Pirlo's journey of self-discovery, even if it meant letting a 16-year-old decide which role fitted best.

In Lucescu's defence, he had a very good understanding of the youngster, and assessed that 'he was a very level-headed guy'. Who, 'as well as being a creative player ... was someone who organised everything' too. So, while it might be unconventional now to relive his days as an attacker, the *Rossoneri* could look at those earlier 'indiscretions' as a lesson from which he would learn and adapt his game. But the pair of them made a more serious transgression in the eyes of the *Milanisti* when Lucescu ended up at Inter and chose to organise a pre-season reserve match against Brescia.

Mario Shenardi, the man eventually drafted in as Pirlo's replacement at Brescia, agrees: 'Pirlo was very lucky to have a coach like Lucescu – he had the intuition that Andrea was a great player.' That much was true. But what should've been a renaissance for the ages of teacher and student with greater stakes at play, turned into a chapter in Lucescu's history books best left ignored.

Background politics and dressing room disagreements shortened Lucescu's term as Inter Milan manager to just 14 games. But that didn't stop him convincing the Inter president to take a punt on bringing Pirlo in after he stood out in that reserve match. He didn't cost that much, so what harm could it do? Well, as it turns out, quite a bit, serving as another unwelcome footnote in the archives of players top clubs have missed out on without trying harder to make things work. Pirlo looked slightly out of his depth in that advanced position under the Inter microscope.

Inter are well known for their creative midfielders. So, there's this expectation which is like a baton passed from new signing to new signing who are tasked with keeping those levels as high as they can. You might hope to catch the media on a good day but playing for a top club can be a poisoned chalice when things aren't going well. If you aren't scoring or creating goals it usually doesn't matter how long you've been there, all they see is an expense that hasn't borne fruit.

Even a mid-season move on loan to Reggina did little to blow air under Pirlo's wings. But his last-minute decision to end the 2000/01 season back with Brescia proved an inspired choice, all thanks to Carlo Mazzone.

Mazzone saw this as an opportunity to see if Andrea Pirlo would fare better based a little further back than what he was used to, so that Roberto Baggio could have free rein. He recognised that playing Baggio and Pirlo in advanced positions made his Brescia side far too top-heavy to sustain any form of stability. Faced with the impossibility of trying to dislodge a determined Baggio from his preferred position, a presumably dejected Pirlo promptly took his station as a defensive midfielder for some regular game time.

Almost instantly, one string in Pirlo's bow took centre-stage – his vision. He displayed a focus which attaches itself to only the most creative and awe-inspiring midfielders of our game. Paul Scholes, Zinedine Zidane, Xavi, Kevin De Bruyne – these are the levels, players who seem to play the game at their own pace, and are always one or two steps ahead of the opposition. They don't wait for the ball to come to them, they find those tiny pockets of space and demand that they receive it there and then. It speaks to that part of the brain which seems to come up with the solution before realising the problem. A solution which usually involves threading the ball through the eye of a needle in order to find its intended target.

Pirlo's talents also lay in his ability to continually, and easily, alter the shape of his team's play. Adopting a drifting technique, he would hit the ball front on with the side of his foot dipped just below its centre of gravity; so as to inject just enough backspin to improve the accuracy of the pass, like a golfer almost deliberately over-clipping their stroke on to the green, to watch it retreat from the bunker and get closer to the hole. Usually, due to the nature of the strike, it's slower, more thoughtful and you'd think easier to intercept. But the quickness of thought that Pirlo used meant it usually evaded the ability of your average defender to intercept it.

Moreover, with someone like Baggio in front of him, he could rest easy knowing that a merely competent ball toward the mercurial striker would likely look a better one. Over the course of the few appearances the pair had together in Brescia there grew an understanding between them which came to a head when Baggio scored a vital late equaliser away against his old side Juventus on 1 April 2001.

Choosing to ignore his improvement, the *Nerazzurri* decided to let Pirlo leave.

Despite not being the first, and most certainly not the last, to make that move from Inter to Milan, Pirlo's move stings harsher than most. Meeting Gennaro Gattuso proved a catalyst in creating what is now recognised as the iconic Pirlo image as a shallow-based orchestral midfielder.

'When I look back now, I realise that I owe everything to Carlo Mazzone and Carlo Ancelotti, the two most important coaches that I've ever had. Under Ancelotti I got right into the role straight away because he trusted me even though he had more experienced players available to him.'

Andrea Pirlo

The fee for Pirlo was somewhere between £15–20m, serious investment for a player who had about ten games' worth of top-flight experience under his belt in the specific role Milan had in mind for him. Even so the then Inter president Massimo Moratti reflected: 'The biggest regret I have had in my career as Inter president was selling Pirlo to Milan. It was my decision to give him away and this was clearly a big mistake.'

One of the more astonishing things I find with Pirlo is how he and Gattuso integrated. Their togetherness, their chemistry and the balance they were able to strike made them a fixture in this Milan side for most of their time together.

With a 'stopper' as enforceable as Gennaro Gattuso, protecting a deep-lying creator as inspiring as Andrea Pirlo, all cultivated under a system liberated by Carlo Ancelotti, it was a symphony of understanding and trust which grew as time progressed. Gattuso earned the ball for Pirlo, Pirlo did whatever he felt like doing, and the world continued to spin. But what if the recipients of Pirlo's passing were not worthy of his efforts? Especially the other two midfielders out of Ancelotti's fluid four? Well, never fear, because the most underrated footballer of his generation is here.

I refer to Clarence Seedorf.

A proud product of one of Ajax's brighter youth churns since the times of Johan Cruyff, Seedorf adopted a symbiotic understanding of the very philosophy which formed the fabric of the Amsterdam club. Since debuting at the age of 16 in the Eredivisie (and becoming the youngest player to do so for Ajax at the time), Seedorf's ascent to the top of the European football pyramid was swift and calculated.

For a side brimming with young, precious talents like Edgar Davids, Jari Litmanen, Patrick Kluivert and Marc Overmars, it would take somebody exceptional to be an exception in that squad. Yet Seedorf's mindset and versatility were key in elevating him to a status above many of his team-mates. Both proved instrumental in maintaining his focus following an early period of success in Holland.

Patrick Kluivert swiped home a late winner against Capello's AC Milan to hand his Ajax cohort an outstanding Champions League triumph in 1995, the third of the titles hoovered by *de Godenzonen* as they went unbeaten for 48 games in the season. It was an accomplishment described by one of many admirers in Real Madrid coach Jorge Valdano, as one 'approaching football utopia'. Tipping his hat to fellow tactician Louis van Gaal, Valdano admitted, 'their concept of the game is exquisite' and noted their 'physical superiority' as being central to their continuance in big games and congested fixture schedules.

Of the many incredible players managed by van Gaal in his distinguished coaching career, I struggle to link many others closer to his philosophies than Clarence Seedorf. 'Football is a team sport and members of the team are dependent on each other,' he said at the time of that final versus Milan. 'If certain players don't carry out their tasks properly on the pitch, then their colleagues will suffer. This means each player must carry out his basic tasks to the best of his ability, and this requires discipline.' Seedorf noticed that van Gaal 'had a very particular philosophy' but that it was for the good of the team. And that was good enough for him.

Seedorf then made an atypical move to Sampdoria, where he shone through the difficulties of having to adapt to the *calcio* culture as an attacking player. There, he embraced the role as a box-to-box midfielder to improve his worth in *I Blucerchiati*'s system and became blood-brothers with Christian Karembeu. Together, the pair proved impossible to displace in their single season together in Sampdoria, and equally impossible to hold on to once Europe's bigger boys showed interest. A common theme in this book so far, another familiar face in Milan's life would reappear at a critical juncture to offer an opportunity a key future component to their success couldn't turn down. It was Fabio Capello, who was interested in drafting both Seedorf and Karembeu to the

Santiago Bernabéu to represent Real Madrid. 'Where are my bags?' responded Seedorf.

It wasn't long before Capello succumbed to the problems brewing in the background at Madrid, but their latest recruit was willing to ignore the earlier scares and grind out a few good personal years in that famous white strip. Meeting the inspiring Fernando Redondo secured Seedorf's focus as that tireless presence beside him. Sometimes he was forced out wide if his physical attributes were needed in less familiar surroundings. His foundation in that 'you need to know how to do everything' Ajax mantra held him in good stead throughout his stay in Spain. He was a key fixture in the teams that earned domestic, continental and intercontinental titles during his three seasons at the club and, barring a fall-out behind the scenes, that could have easily been extended. However, a number of unsalvageable discussions around a potential new contract slapped a 'for sale' sign on his back. Looking back on his time in Spain, Real Madrid themselves have been uncharacteristically vocal in their admiration for their ex-employee. Their official website reads: 'Clarence Seedorf is one of Europe's most complete midfielders of the last few decades.' They call him 'a great competitor' and 'a force of nature' in an epitaph entitled, 'A privileged physique and refined skill'.

Though he would leave Madrid with gritted teeth, Seedorf would be offered an enticing prospect back in Italy. This time he would be draped in the colours of the *Nerazzurri* with the names Ronaldo and Vieri to look at all game long. In what was promised as a high-end ticket to the pinnacle of European football with long-term contracts and smart investment all round, it would turn out to be an episode described by their latest acquisition as 'short, but amazing'. Two seasons later, most would be forgiven for thinking that Clarence was older than he actually was. A homegrown *'Invincible'*, he had won two European Cups and two domestics league titles in separate countries – most would be fortunate to earn one of those achievements through the entirety of their career, let alone at just 26 years old. But, as we know, Inter have a history of overlooking the promise in their squad when their stadium brothers come calling.

Seedorf was signed by AC Milan for a small fee plus Francesco Coco on a three-year deal ahead of the 2002/03 season. Patrick Goss, the former Sky Sports reporter, wrote at the time that, considering Inter's long-felt position of wanting to offload the seemingly expensive Seedorf, and the stock taken up on the prospect that Coco was back then, 'neither San Siro side will feel they have got a bad deal'.

> 'For me, winning isn't just about lifting the cup, the trophy – it's about giving your maximum, on and off the pitch.'
>
> *Clarence Seedorf*

Seedorf's arrival was like adding a layer of polish to an already sophisticated and sturdy Milan midfield. With him they were practically impenetrable. In order of approach, you'd have to be pretty quick, strong and innovative to force your way past. Seedorf was now fully versed in the art of tracking the ball from one penalty area to the other; Pirlo, though not your average cruncher, would find his abilities shone when given the ball in the smallest of spaces. Lose control of that ball for a moment and you're not getting it back. But if you keep your footing well enough, then you're treated to a salivating Gattuso. A man who would mow you down first and ask questions later.

An area none of these players excelled in, however, was all-out attack. Sure, they could create and shoot if they really needed to, but their roles were really to get the fundamentals correct so that the final man in the midfield four didn't have to. The good news was Carlo Ancelotti knew exactly the type of man he would need to improve the production value of his midfield. The bad news? He'd have to walk down a painful alleyway on memory lane to do it. That's right. He needed a *trequartista*.

Thankfully for everyone associated with Milan at the time, Ancelotti adapted well when he realised how wrong he had been until then.

Though largely successful at Reggina and Parma, there's always a sense of what could have been through the glasses of retrospect. What if he was more adventurous with his selection? What if he took more risks when his side were in possession? Most importantly: what if he took the plunge to see how his side would fare outside of his favourite formation? But alas, that flat four in midfield was believed to be the way forward for his young and hungry side who, in his opinion, would be in a position to outwork some of their opponents if they were unmatched technically and creatively. At Parma, this proved twice to be a particularly poor decision.

Ostracising both Gianfranco Zola and Roberto Baggio still remain among his poorer decisions in a generally glittering career. I'll leave the debate over who was the better player, but whatever the choice, either was unequivocally valuable enough to remain with Ancelotti longer than they did.

This time a more learned Ancelotti was willing to throw real resources behind this headhunting project, and he didn't even need to look far; Fatih Terim's proudest acquisition, Rui Costa, proved the perfect rehearsal partner.

There's a common phrase thrown about on Twitter nowadays; 'that guy knows ball'. A colloquialism used to flatter your everyday fan who thinks about the game a little more deeply than most. The kind of person who wishes OptaStats would grant an honorary assist to the guy who dummies the ball through their legs to give the forward extra space to get the shot away, rather than to the original sender who gets one added to their list out of courtesy. The guys who know ball tend to think that players deserve more credit for all the things they're capable of which fly under the radar. Their stats might not be high enough to earn a Ballon d'Or – but they have our hearts, and that's what matters.

There are three substantial contributing factors: selflessness, humility and liberty in the way they play. Rui Costa slots seamlessly into each of these. He was underpinned by an outstanding level of loyalty which permeated his ability to be great at what he did.

The genesis of Costa's playing career derived from the welcoming setting of Benfica, a club well known for their proud, illustrious European history.

Costa soon hit the glass ceiling above the most bright Benfica players and packed his bags for Fiorentina. He arrived with the toughness and self-awareness of someone who knew they were talented, but equally that they'd have to prove it again to be loved once more. It didn't take long for him to be the biggest attraction in purple since Prince in the 80s.

Some *Viola* fans might flinch at him being given a headliner's spot over his team-mates. Fiery front man Gabriel Batistuta is usually everybody's choice. Interestingly, the difference between the two serves as a good example per my 'knowing ball' reference. Batistuta's name works as a phonetic expression of the type of player he was.

The lovingly named 'Batigol' was a revelation wherever he went during his playing career, with arguably his best years coming in Florence. He wasn't understated. His aim was to be noticed, to be feared, revered and respected by anybody who watched him – and scoring a bunch of goals, to a point where it influences your nickname, is a surefire way of making that happen. But, even a casual fan can scour an old stats book and realise that Batistuta was a top striker. As for the playmaker stationed behind him, only those who 'know ball' are able to look beyond the numbers to admire the lurking Costa.

Batistuta was the lead singer, but Costa wrote the song and they combined to produce something beautiful.

Costa's Florentine wizardry lasted the better part of seven seasons, arguably leading to him becoming their most treasured player when Batistuta left for Rome in 2000. His dedication to the cause wilted under the pressure of the club's financial problems until the most helpful thing he could do was leave for a bigger fee than Bati's.

Depressingly, Milan fans were robbed of an in-form, confident and free-flowing Rui Costa. A player as personally reputable, fair and committed as he deserved to enjoy an unequivocally successful time at such a big club. But football isn't fair, and two outside influences in particular thwarted a steady route into the hearts of Milanese fans: club instability and personal injury. A lack of the latter could have helped to quell the impact of the former, but it just wasn't meant to be. Having said that, for the limited number of appearances he did have in front of the San Siro faithful, he did well enough to earn a slot in the Milan Hall of Fame once he retired, where he's described as a 'remarkable number ten' despite his unremarkable goals/assists tally across nearly 200 appearances in red and black.

Ancelotti's side was now *so* good, that it opened a space for an unadulterated, unfiltered, unwavering chance-maker to strut his stuff and give those fans their money's worth, a player who could pick up some of those positions Costa made home, but would then have the permission to plough further forward in aid of the forwards. Therefore, somebody confident, young and ignorant of fear would be the recommended formula.

Ancelotti's target was – and I use this word sparingly – perfect.

> 'He's young and extremely talented. He will face tough competition in his position but he's ready to work alongside players like Rui Costa. He will not be cover for them – he will be in competition with them for a place in the side.'
>
> *Carlo Ancelotti*

The player to whom Ancelotti turned was Kaká. A delightful anecdote from his extraordinary career is where his name came from. According to the man himself – whose passport bears the forename of 'Ricardo' – his younger brother had difficulty pronouncing his name as a toddler. So, instead of learning the art of putting more than two syllables together, he spouted 'Kaká'. The player found the innocence of it very touching and he allowed it to form part of his image, deciding to keep it when offered his first professional football contract in Sao Paulo.

Exploding on to the local scene, he took on a form emblematic of the conflicting aspects of his personal life. More specifically, the political and social uncertainty of the world around him, and the peaceful, serene feeling of security brought on by his deep faith in Christianity. I may be being hyperbolic but I've seldom noticed much fear in Kaká's game. It's as if he played with the feeling of knowing that there was something greater than him making sure he was going to be safe in whatever he tried, or even that some of his more exuberant efforts were going to be successful if he had faith that they were going to happen as he intended. Then, knowing where he came from and the life from which he was looking to lead his family away ensured that he went about his work knowing the importance of what he was trying to do; to use football as his God-given springboard.

You never got the impression that football was just a job for Kaká. It was more a calling, something he was born to do. And that passion bled into how he carried himself as a professional player, which is what made him so likeable and relatable to the Brazilian people.

A key business partner to Berlusconi and Ancelotti, Adriano Galliani was an instrumental figure in waving away external advances for the Brazilian, and drafting in Kaká for his own needs. He even remembers having to remove another squad member to prioritise his new signing under UEFA's limited rules on registering non-EU players. Apparently, the club were even willing to continue paying the wages of their outgoer if it meant that the governing body recognised Kaká as theirs. The proud Galliani places the attacker's legacy alongside the likes of Maldini and Baresi; in that 'it is probably fair to say that the fans' affection for Kaká is equally big'.

The unfortunate unreliability of an ageing Rui Costa opened the door to signing Kaká earlier than most could have anticipated. Ignoring a storybook return in the twilight years of his career, Kaká spent only two full seasons in the all-white of Sao Paulo before trading it for those famous red and black stripes. Which could have been a disastrous foundation for the impending career that he'd build.

On reflection, he and goalkeeper Dida were in a strikingly similar scenario upon their entrances into the San Siro. Both had a number of impressive displays on home soil to give reason they would succeed at a higher level, but they were tasked with roles which needed filling properly, consistently and immediately. Dida flourished under the weight of expectation, as did Kaká; and then some.

As part of his installation process, he and Costa were used in rotation in the Brazilian's maiden season in Italy. The latter's physical failings contrasted significantly with the former's youthful bloom to soon make Kaká the first choice for that position. For while Costa maintained, and might have even improved upon, his wealth of technical strengths to caress the ball and push it lovingly toward its new owner, that brash, primitive ability to threaten the opposition wilted with age. As did, or so it appeared, his prime levels of confidence to trust his body to put his instincts into action.

So, in typically humble and putting-the-team-first fashion, Costa became an honorary mentor in supporting the early developments of Kaká to become AC Milan's star man. It was a tutelage which proved vital in improving the Brazilian's decision-making skills once he got into the final third. Galliani, a shameless admirer of Costa, recalls the Portuguese's benign reaction to observing Kaká in training. 'He is better than me,' whispered Costa, much to Galliani's surprise. Accurate or not, including his successor in his all-time XI in an interview with *GOAL* in 2016 speaks loudly of the pair's relationship. As it does of how this kid was able to acclimatise to his new and intimidating surroundings so quickly.

He might have at first experienced a form of imposter syndrome on that pitch, with those players and under those expectations. Simply being a flashy player capable of the extraordinary every now and again was never going to cut it. In order to survive, he needed to be consistent. Fortunately in his earlier seasons the midfield on which he perched himself allowed him to be as expressive as he wanted. While learning the art of staying focused and professional at the same time, they all got used to each other very quickly. Now that area of the pitch pretty much had everything it needed, and I struggle to remember a midfield four better suited to each other than this one.

Altogether, Milan's quartet was the epitome of hard work and technical balance. At its base, you have the industrious workhorse of Gennaro Gattuso. Complementing his tenacity, is the ability of Andrea Pirlo to see clearly what needed to happen next. For that injection of energy, there was Clarence Seedorf to force open the door.

Then, around 70–80 per cent into the route to a goalscoring opportunity, they would find Kaká. The four operated like a well-tuned orchestra in the grandest theatre the world has ever seen, with goosebump-inducing levels of performance that make it hard to cast your mind to another group that was as awe-inspiring as they were. The dedication, the precision, the invention. In playing the way they did and producing the moments they have they rightly stake their claim in Milan's own memory bank of truly great midfield players.

I can only imagine that the excitement of working with them only slightly outweighed the trepidation growing inside Carlo Ancelotti when it came to picking his strikers. How do you possibly find a good enough cherry to top this extraordinary cake? The layers, the textures, the taste.

Milan had grown used to having top strikers in the past. George Weah and Marco van Basten are among my favourites. Both won the Ballon d'Or and many who followed failed to live up to their level.

CHAPTER EIGHT

'The Finishing Touches'

FOR THOSE who have some idea of the different approaches to *futbol* in South America than with most areas of the world, you would align its inherent elegance and poise with the emergence of Hernán Crespo as a River Plate marksman.

River Plate – as well as tense connections with other local teams – has a particularly incendiary relationship with fellow trophy-hoggers, Boca Juniors. Now, we'd have to cut down the Amazon to produce the amount of paper needed to fully explain why, but for want of simplicity, their playing styles each reflect their inner ways of living. Opposing Boca's 'by any means' focus, River are all about the aesthetics – winning a game 'in the right way'. Sure, the result may still be the same regardless of the tactics chosen to get there, but the self-righteousness is palpable. Put it this way: I'd imagine that Gennaro Gattuso would perfectly suit Boca, whereas Andrea Pirlo would be a prime fit for the fans of River. The long hair helps, too.

For all intents and purposes, Crespo was your typical River Plate striker in the way he looked and his natural game plan. Crespo was the man Ancelotti signed twice.

He had struggled initially when Ancelotti took him to Parma from River in 1996. Strictly speaking, he'd barely grown much of his stock back home by the time he was on a plane to Italy. The return of club icon Enzo Francescoli couldn't have helped matters but stats will be stats.

He relied on the intuition and backing of his manager to plough through the early rain clouds and into the clear. From November in his maiden campaign, his weight of goalscoring was there for all to see. After that he averaged nearly a goal a game. Crespo would spend four years at Parma and cast aside any original doubts with every passing strike. His success was enough to see Ancelotti earn a bigger move to Juve while Crespo stayed put, a decision which was not forgotten by the die-hard, unrelenting *I Crociati* support.

Back to his younger self, he was eventually seduced by that all-star Lazio squad. The very same one that Nesta and Stam were brought into at the time. While there, Crespo became the operative cause behind Lazio's success, finishing his inaugural season in sky blue with 39 goals in 54 games to largely repay his world record transfer from Parma, a cash-plus-players deal believed to be around £35 million.

After Lazio's financial troubles sent him to Inter Milan, where he played only 18 games, he was off to Chelsea where he scored 20 times in 49 games.

But then José Mourinho arrived at Stamford Bridge and Crespo was replaced by Marseille's Didier Drogba.

Crespo returned to Italy and a loan deal with AC Milan.

'I need tranquillity because I have two motivations; first the wish to stay here

permanently and secondly the need to
score as soon as possible.'

Hernán Crespo shortly after joining AC Milan
on loan in 2004

Ancelotti must have had Crespo's maturing
qualities in mind and it was not only a chance
to play for a club he long admired, but it was a
reunion with a man he so trusted. 'When you have
problems, you always go back to your parents,' said
Crespo. 'My football father is Carlo Ancelotti.'
However, in an interview with a reporter from *La
Gazzetta Dello Sport*, Galliani confessed that he
had to be won over. But he stated that Carlo was
the manager and he believed in his ability to pick
and choose the right players to fit into his playing
system, if only for a short time.

The man who had been in main possession
of the AC Milan striker's jersey had been at the
San Siro since joining them from Dynamo Kyiv
in 1999. And in that time Andriy Shevchenko had
proved himself one of the best in the world.

'When I was a child, it was my dream to
be a professional footballer. When I was

14, I visited Milan's San Siro stadium and remember thinking how unbelievable it was. From then onwards I vowed that one day I would be playing there – and I am very proud that I achieved this and also for everything else I have managed to achieve in football.'

Andriy Shevchenko

Shevchenko's performance against Barcelona in the Champions League and, of course, his form at home in Ukraine prompted then Milan sporting director Arieldo Braida to drag his unconvinced CEO Galliani to Kiev on a scouting mission. Shevchenko admits that they did not witness his best performance – in fact, he called it 'hideous' in an interview in 2021. But he was thankful that Braida had done his homework and decided to persist with his mission to sign him. 'He saw something in me that I didn't even know I had,' reads Shevchenko's characteristically humble account. 'And when he came to my house to convince me to sign, he gave me a *Rossoneri* shirt with my name on it. "You will win the Ballon d'Or with this one," he told me. My father and I laughed.

'But he was right.'

Five years later Shevchenko was officially declared the best-performing player in world football by FIFA. In doing so, he became the first player from his country to win that honour, joining a very exclusive list of great AC Milan players to do the same.

From my generation, he is, statistically, one of the best strikers in his time. The numbers equally favour Thierry Henry, David Trezeguet and Ruud van Nistelrooy but that's a good list to be on.

History places Andriy Shevchenko firmly on the shelf reserved for players like these, almost solely for the aura of inevitability he was able to cultivate at his best. He was a member of the elite group of football players with whom there was an expectation that the net would ripple when they got it in their sights.

The following also deserve a mention: Kakha Kaladze, the rough Georgian centre-back who arrived from Kyiv to reunite with Shevchenko the year after he'd left; Vikash Dhorasoo, a largely unused midfielder who helped boost the squad; Serginho, the ultimate utility man and a rare breed of midfielder good enough in defence should his manager require it. He had a pretty decent engine in him as well; hence his occasional use as a makeshift full-back.

And finally there was Jon Dahl Tomasson; a forward defined by effort and discipline.

But now you maybe thinking, why stop there?

After all, these aren't the *only* players Carlo Ancelotti managed during his time at AC Milan. The answer is very simple. These were all selected to take part in one of, if not the most, infamous moments in the club's history, a UEFA Champions League Final fixture on 25 May 2005.

Hereafter known as, 'The Nightmare in Istanbul'.

CHAPTER NINE

'The Journey to Hell'

THIS ISN'T going to be a very pleasant section to read for Milan fans, so let's start with something a little brighter, probably the most memorable notch on Ancelotti's European belt, the victory in the the UEFA Champions League back in 2003.

The final failed to live up to the expectations set by both sides throughout the tournament. Domestic foes Juventus were in particularly free-flowing form prior to meeting Milan at Old Trafford to settle who won the title that year. But when the two Italian heavyweights came to blows, it went to the judges' scorecards. Well, penalties, but I wanted to continue with the boxing analogy. Reporter Paul Milton from the *Guardian* concluded that 'based on that much, I'd say reports of the revival of Italian football are greatly exaggerated'. Slightly harsh, perhaps though his 'poor passing and dire finishing' remark was fair.

Looking back, Milan could consider themselves unlucky to have a goal disallowed in the first half. Had VAR been in existence then their head office would have been all over the referee's call for an offside against Rui Costa for obstructing Buffon's view of Shevchenko's shot after seven minutes. The woodwork was also struck a couple of times before the game completely lost its momentum in the second half, both sides appearing to fear a late loss rather than focusing on trying to get a late winner. Extra time followed that same recipe before penalties loomed. Milton's joke prediction of the shoot-out ending 0-0 like the rest of the game was laid to rest, although each goalkeeper could be happy with their respective efforts, even if Dida ventured about three yards off the goal line to narrow down the angle. Again, VAR might have had something to say about that.

Inevitably Shevchenko slotted home the decisive spot kick to take the trophy to Milan. A win that all fans would claim but would take some time to remember. It wasn't the way they usually earned European glory and the whole occasion seemed more the opposite of great, attractive football than the legacy of the AC Milan teams with which they would have been happy to align. But a win is a win the saying goes, even if it wasn't much of a story. But not to worry, they'd have a great opportunity to put any negative press to rest by the time the 2004/05 version of the tournament came around. Okay, *Milanisti*, you have been warned ...

Milan saw themselves drawn in Group F alongside Barcelona, Shakhtar Donetsk and Celtic, which, barring miracles from Ukraine and Scotland, would be considered 'favourable' by most. But Barca, though a couple of years away from assembling arguably the most synergistic club side of all time, were a force to be reckoned with, especially under the guidance of Milan hero Frank Rijkaard, who brought as much as he could out of the Ronaldinho and Samuel Eto'o partnership.

Even then, Ancelotti's men did their best to ensure that the forthcoming steps of the competition were as welcoming as possible by finishing top of the group. I use the word 'welcoming' loosely, only because it meant that by heading up their bunch, they'd now face a side who were runners-up in theirs. So, what was their reward? After scoring 13 points from a possible 18 they faced a two-game affair with Sir Alex Ferguson's Manchester United in the round of 16.

> 'It's an extremely difficult game for us …
> I hope we get a really top performance because we're going to need one.'
>
> *- Sir Alex Ferguson before facing Milan in*
> *March 2005*

These European titans had enjoyed their own variety of success since their last elite cup match-up in the late 60s, though Ferguson's unusually reserved preview of their latest challenge forebode positive things for the Italian side.

Rather fortunately for Milan, United appeared hungover from a number of transitional years since the turn of the millennium. This wasn't the all-conquering side that won the treble in 99, nor were they the team who finished second to Guardiola's

Barcelona between 2007–10. They were somewhere in between, and ripe for exposure at the back so long as Milan were clued in on how and when to reveal those opportunities.

In the first of two matches against the English giants, Ancelotti shrewdly chose to go with two attacking midfielders instead of the one he would play in the final – presumably to combat United's depth of quantity in the same area. The movements and guile of Rui Costa and Kaká were enough to break the home team's resolve as Crespo gained his side a crucial away goal to take back to the San Siro, where, despite almost everything changing – the setting, the setup of United this time round and the stakes for what would happen if they didn't show up – the result was exactly the same. AC Milan 1 Manchester United 0 (2-0 on aggregate).

Even dovetailing the fledgling stars of Cristiano Ronaldo and Wayne Rooney with the likes of Giggs, Scholes and van Nistelrooy, proved futile in accessing Milan's impregnable goalmouth, something which the single-minded Dutch forward remembered well when asked about the nature of Italian defences in a live interview at the

Oxford Union in 2016. The audience laughed at Ruud's wincing face as he recalled the names he had to face in the tie. With a wry smile and a tilt of the head, he rustled up enough courage to call the experience 'interesting', while confessing that they were 'pretty good', also.

In truth, it wasn't even that much of a negative performance from Milan; they knew where and when to pick and go for their moments in the match. Which I would argue was more to do with the collective intelligence of the players than an instruction from the manager to shut out United and hope for the best at the opposite end. They might not have got away with it against another Italian side but it would have been easier against an opponent not accustomed to the Italian way.

But their next match would be a different issue; a grudge affair with blood-brothers Inter Milan. That's always a noteworthy fixture, but on this occasion it was a gold-lettered page in one of world football's most incestuous, intriguing and thought-provoking rivalries.

For reasons unlike any other, the Derby Della Madonnina is an almighty spectacle, one that morphs the issues of proximity, jealousy and success all into one.

The political difference which split the two Milan clubs during their early years tipped the balance of aristocracy in favour of Inter, although this would erode over time. Legendary players, media magnates, gambling issues and an openness to foreign policies have seen these two battle it out to be dubbed the best team in the country. Maldini, a man who played in 56 such derbies, the most on either side, described the significance of the event. 'It was always a great thrill,' he said, though 'there were [also] various emotions.'

Strangely, when asked about the fixture in a 2019 interview, he responded in a way which almost told the story of the auspicious voyage through the 2004/05 Champions League. 'Perhaps the most exciting of all were those of the Champions League: winning a semi-final played in six days, round trip, qualify for the final and then win the cup. In the end it is the result that counts, probably the most intense ones.'

Though I would not put Inter's team on a par with the specific manpower at Milan's disposal from this period, I admit that they employed some of my favourite footballers.

He played up top, *Il Emperor.* The one and only Adriano.

The story of Adriano, one of Brazil's most explosive strikers, was certainly one of football's saddest 'what if?' tales. Inter had taken a punt on the youngster when he was breaking through at Flamengo, but it wasn't until a co-ownership setup with Parma revealed the best of what he had to offer.

He was electric … absolutely electric. Quick, forward-thinking, uncompromising – a player who quickly proved worthy of carrying the baton passed on by Brazil's top forwards. And but for a life-altering nine days there's enough cause to reason that he would have been one of the best that ever lived.

The Players' Tribune published in 2021 the most insightful account of Adriano's story that I've read. I suggest there as the destination to properly demystify what you might think about the ex-Inter frontman. I prefer to remember how good he truly was in his prime.

To begin with, Milan's culture and intelligence seemed to overwhelm a constantly changing and unsettled Inter, as they achieved a 2-0 shutout in favour of the 'home side'. Disruption to the status quo would be needed to overturn that deficit, though I don't believe that either team had that in mind.

> 'What happened will not just discredit Inter but all of the city. The reaction of the Inter fans was completely unexpected. I was really surprised because I have never seen something like that in all of the Milan derbies that I have taken part in. Now we have to refocus on football so that people can calm down after this disgraceful episode.'
>
> *Carlo Ancelotti's post-second-leg reaction in*
> *2005*

For a while, it did appear business would be as usual when a 30th-minute strike from Andriy Shevchenko took the tie further out of Inter's grasp. It meant, with the away rule in effect, they would technically need four goals. An opening presented itself when Esteban Cambiasso thought he clawed back some semblance of dignity by tapping the ball beyond Dida with about 20 minutes to go. That is, until the referee's whistle shattered any hope given how much time was left.

In retrospect, I think most will agree that it was a soft call to pull back play for a supposed push from a non-scorer in the build-up. Had today's scope of technology been available for use, then this goal would have stood.

Instead, the decision was too much for the spectators in blue to bear. Such was their disgust – as well as his decision to book Cambiasso for dissent – that they took their display of dissatisfaction to an unacceptable level. The use of a flare, though not uncommon in most parts of central European football, was grossly misused by a number of Inter fans. Transcripts from the stands that evening describe the sheer scale of flares there were among the crowd, and how they largely made for a rough and unsafe atmosphere for most of the match. Things, quite literally, got out of hand. Milan police chief Paolo Scarpi said 'there were two or three hundred hooligans who were involved in throwing the flares', and he promised that they'd been caught on camera and would be punished to the fullest extent of the law. He admitted that most perpetrators 'were the usual hotheads from the Inter sector' while the country's interior minister Giuseppe Pisano's prior warning that 'intolerable' behaviour was known and needed addressing, would come as little consolation to all affected victims.

Milan's goalkeeper Dida was the worst affected by the flares. A lit torch was thrown in Dida's direction and struck the broad Brazilian square in the face. After which, like a heavyweight fighter felled by a Tyson left hook and uppercut combo, gravity took hold – knocking him to the ground and the game to a halt. The poor lad suffered first-degree burns because of the incident, and was lucky to not sustain further, long-term damage to either of his eyes.

Play was permanently stopped, Inter took a forfeit and UEFA credited Milan with a 3-0 win for their troubles. Days after, Inter were ordered to play their next six European games behind closed doors, and were fined around £132,000. The director of communications for UEFA at the time, William Gaillard, appeared content while reviewing these penalties, boasting that 'this is the highest fine in the history of UEFA and the loss of four home games will mean they lose out on revenue of around €8 million'. While true, I'd argue that prohibiting European contention the following year would have been the better punishment, but that would indirectly hurt the governors too.

The year 2020 (among many other things) marked the 15-year point following this infamous edition of the derby, with social media outlets like *Bleacher Report*, *Sporf* and UEFA themselves remembering the iconic shots taken from that day. Of them all, there's one which remains in my memory. It shows Inter's Marco Materazzi leaning on the shoulder of Milan's Rui Costa as they look on without discussion at the anarchy before them. However, while Materazzi's thoughts were riddled with despondency in knowing that Inter would have to face the music, Costa and his team-mates could at least look forward to a semi-final against PSV Eindhoven.

In the first leg a toothless Eindhoven were powerless to overcome Milan. Starter Shevchenko and sub Jon Dahl Tomasson combined to give their side a 2-0 advantage going into the away leg, the preamble to which was a pretty mixed bag of analysis. The lazier journalists believed that Milan would put the tie to bed early on and amble their way into the tournament decider. The glass-half-empty writers reckoned Milan were lucky to keep a clean sheet in the first leg and were susceptible to counter-attacks. The most daring drew comparisons with the previous season's capitulation in the European quarter-finals against Deportivo de La Coruña. Milan had won 4-1 at home only to be humbled 4-0 days later to give the Spaniards the tie on aggregate. PSV would need, at the very least, to start well; and start well they did.

A slick move through the heart of Milan ended with fan-favourite Ji-Sung Park flashing a low drive past Dida with barely ten minutes on the clock. From which point, the wind was firmly in PSV's sails as they looked to overcome Milan's technical superiority. Their centre-backs made sure Shevchenko and Kaká enjoyed as little fun as possible, even if it meant taking the odd knock here or there to make sure they didn't get through. At the opposite end, the tireless Park and effervescent Jefferson Farfán were not respecting their maturing opponents. Ancelotti even felt the need to preserve Maldini from another half of potential embarrassment in favour of Kaladze instead. But even that didn't do the trick.

With the aid of marauding wing-back Young-Pyo Lee, PSV again invaded enemy territory to set up a simple header for veteran midfielder Phillip Cocu, who, having claimed that 'Milan are beatable' on the eve of the match, would have enjoyed that equaliser more than most. Cocu's header goaded Ancelotti into taking unorthodox measures to stop the bleeding. Seedorf was removed to reintroduce a familiar PSV antagonist from the first match, Tomasson, to formalise a change in tactics for Milan to a by any means necessary approach in search of a winner. And it was midfielder Massimo Ambrosini who stepped up to stick a dagger into the home side on the 90th-minute mark, sliding a competent effort beyond Gomes, the flailing PSV goalkeeper. Not even an extra piece of magic from Cocu was enough to affect the away goals mountain, and so Milan would advance to the final in unfamiliar circumstances. Some believed that they were unworthy.

Mark van Bommel recounted: 'When you play two games better than AC Milan you deserve to win, but they scored the away goal, which is the most important thing. We were the best team. It was a sucker punch.' His coach, Guus Hiddink, kept the blame in-house: 'We were very, very close until the last minute and then we threw it all away.'

Whatever slant you put on it, it was a warning signal that on-paper ability isn't a guarantee to see you through a side that wants it more, a factor Ancelotti would need to take into account following confirmation that they would face Liverpool in the final, a side with about as many chasms in their team as he had reinforcements in his.

CHAPTER TEN

'Istanbul'

'I can't explain it.'

Carlo Ancelotti

NEITHER CAN I, Carlo. Neither can I.

That's football for you though, isn't it? At times, beautiful and by nature, completely inexplicable.

We do know that both Milan and Liverpool had enjoyed European knockout football in the past. Milan had won the trophy six times, more than any other Italian club, while Liverpool had won one fewer, but more than any other club in England.

Coming into the final at the Atatürk Olympic Stadium in Istanbul, Liverpool hadn't won since

1984, and had largely neglected many of the elements which formed the basis of those winning teams. Bill Shankly, an iconic figure largely credited with building the Reds into one of England's proudest institutions, envisioned a world where Liverpool FC carried themselves better than any other around them. Stacked among thousands of other soundbites from the revolutionary Scotsman, was this: 'My idea was to build Liverpool into a bastion of invincibility. Had Napoleon had that idea he would have conquered the bloody world. I wanted Liverpool to be untouchable ... to build [them] up and up until eventually everyone would have to submit and give in.'

Bob Paisley, statistically Liverpool's most successful ever manager with 20 trophies in roughly nine years in charge, considered it an honour to align his best achievements with the team that had 'been [his] life', insisting that 'I'd go out and sweep the street and be proud to do it for Liverpool FC if they asked me to.' It will come as no surprise to anyone that having a strong technical outfit is key to enjoying anywhere near the glamour they had during this era of Merseyside dominance. But that desire to work hard: for yourself, each other and the fans who fork out their hard-earned cash to watch you, is the superseding motivator for it all.

Since those days, however, cyclical factors had caused this once-great Liverpool team to lose their way. Ownership struggles, financial tussles and recruitment grumbles permeated on to the pitch and wreaked havoc with the side's consistency. It was such that they came into the 2004/05 season in search of their first English league title for 15 years. But they were still Liverpool, still one of the world's biggest clubs. They were still capable of the incredible, much like their unofficial treble feat of 2000/01. Derisively remembered as an inferior selection of trophies relative to the 'big stuff' by rival supporters, but heralded by at least 500,000 of their own through the streets of Liverpool.

That us against them mentality resonated closely with the then manager Rafael Benítez, a pragmatic coach whose premature, ended playing days added to a weighty managerial portfolio since he began as Real Madrid's U17 coach in 1986.

Those youth lessons in Madrid, a stop-over in Osasuna and sun-soaked periods in Tenerife rendered an advancing move to Valencia a 'surprise'. Yet, despite not being their first choice (or third, for that matter), Benítez's rotational preferences and chance-taking transfer policy made him a fine appointment in retrospect. Finer still, twice becoming Spanish champions and even a European winner having scooped up a UEFA Cup title against Marseille in 2004, thrust his Valencia side firmly up the Spanish football ladder, a near impossibility considering the Barca/Real duopoly, which continues to dominate to this day. But for a few differences of opinion, Rafa and Valencia would have had even longer to chip away at their defences, and who knows where they would have ended. But alas, the tearful Spaniard was moved to make 'one of the most difficult decisions I've had to make in my sporting life'.

Among his suitors was a rudderless Liverpool in desperate need of direction. The tail-end of the departing term under Gérard Houllier was a mixed bag, and heavily impeded Rafa's immediate plans for the transfer market. Growing fears throughout the season of torn ties and strained relationships with some of the club's longer-term servants were realised, with almost 20 senior players leaving the Anfield dressing room that summer, chief among them Michael Owen and Emile Heskey, a fruitful striking partnership.

Regardless of the difficulties predicted by many, Benítez held close to the formula that put him into the limelight back home. While he did ultimately use the money given to him and plugged gaps as he saw fit, his 'experience, youth, enthusiasm' trifecta comprised his most used XI through that first season. That equation wasn't enough to get them higher than fifth in the league but it was the key to confidence in Europe.

The words 'oh, you beauty ... what a hit son, what a hit' rounded out an insecure group stage experience for Benítez's men. But fortunately, that goosebump-inducing moment from captain Steven Gerrard propelled them into the round of 16, before they despatched an overwhelmed Bayer Leverkusen side 6-2 on aggregate.

Liverpool would only score half as many across their next four fixtures, but they picked their times well. Twice in front of an electric Anfield crowd against Juve before a shut-out in Italy.

Then it happened once more when the ball broke fortuitously toward the boot of Luis García, who prodded the ball centimetres beyond the line against Chelsea. At least, that's how the home support made it look, as the roar of the Merseyside crowd seemed to marry well with García's performance to convince the officials to give the goal. Now added to a line of infamous 'ghost goals', the Spanish forward offers his own satirical account of what happened in that third minute. 'My reaction to the goal is straightforward,' began his address. 'I don't wait around, I just run off to celebrate. My reaction means I saw the ball going in. Nothing more to say, your honour.' An airtight Liverpool held bravely on to that early advantage to take 40,000 supporters along for the ride to Turkey.

> 'People say we were one of the worst teams to win [the Champions League], and they're right, we were one of the worst.'
>
> *Jamie Carragher*

Other commentary appears to concur with Carragher's self-effacing view of his Liverpool side compared to their opponents. You be the judge:

While Milan's Dida patrolled one goalmouth, Jerzy Dudek looked after the other. Cafu; the definition of consistency and stability on the right flank found competition in Steve Finnan. Maldini's a tough gig at the worst of times but even at his best, Djimi Traoré wasn't a worthy comparison. But the comparison at centre-back was much closer. Stam and Nesta were in a class of their own but their yin-yang feature is loosely reminiscent of the differences between Jamie Carragher and Sami Hyypiä. Carragher was a passionate, uncompromising man who would bleed for the badge if required, while Hyppiä would administer a dressing to his wounds with surgical precision. I'd go as far as to call the Finnish international the best pound-for-pound Liverpool centre-half of his time.

Oddly enough, the midfield battle follows a similar recipe – moreish on the inside with a rough aftertaste on the outside. Xabi Alonso was a beautiful footballer, who must curse his luck at being born into the same era as Xavi, Iniesta and Busquets. On his own, the silky Spaniard could salsa his way into most teams as a deep-lying playmaker. Equally his dance partner, Steven Gerrard, probably the most well-rounded English midfielder of his generation, could have tailgated him.

When I think of the key characteristics I want to see in a midfield marshal – leadership, passing range, threat on goal, non-stop drive, boundless energy, love for the cause – Steven Gerrard just slightly outranks his fellow midfielders from the beginning of his career through to its end in 2016.

Coming into the final, both he and Xabi Alonso were nearing the peak of their powers in a Liverpool shirt, and could have even made it into that AC Milan team with a droplet of good fortune. Just don't ask me who to leave out.

Unlike Benítez, Ancelotti didn't feel the need to have typical wingers in his side, so it's difficult to make a like-for-like comparison as we've done so far. Technically, Luis García was quicker than Kaká, and John Arne Riise might have possessed a left foot more explosive than Seedorf's right. But even both of these opinions are given with the benefit of my doubt. There isn't any of that when it comes to the forwards.

It speaks to the strength of Milan that Crespo is the closest there was to a weak link. Yet he meshes in well enough with Shevchenko to appear an inspired inclusion. I can't say the same for Harry Kewell or Milan Baroš. Kewell was exceptional as a Leeds winger during the preliminary stages of his Premier League career, one of those players who, when they were playing for a mid-table side, was the type you'd say deserved a transfer to a bigger club. But it never quite worked out for him after he moved to Merseyside. By contrast, Baroš, even at his best, was an okay striker. Nostalgia might add the occasional sparkle to a generally insubstantial career in England, but his energy and sprightliness would at least form a barrier to his lack of technical quality in facing a side like Milan.

So, to sum up: a goalkeeper fit for a highlight reel, a defence threatening to leak more heavily than Old Trafford in a monsoon, a midfield with a whiff of potential about it and a strike force made with a built-in whiff extinguisher. But Benítez was no fool. He would have studiously assessed his squad's depth to pick out what was needed for the task, and equip them with the policies required to make it a reality. It wouldn't surprise me if he'd banked on his side winning the opening toss to kick things off with the wind blowing in their direction. In any event, Baroš rolled the ball into Kewell (this was before referees allowed a solitary kick-off starter), who tapped the ball into midfield. Thus was set in motion one of the most notable matches in European history.

Traoré landed himself in hot water from the get-go by allowing Kaká to get the run on him with 30 seconds on the clock. The Malian then saw no option but to bring down the Brazilian which offered Pirlo the first opportunity of the match to swing an unopposed ball into the Liverpool 18-yard box. Thinking outside said box (pun intended), Pirlo led his side through what looked like a set-piece training exercise. Instead of lumping in a cross toward the usual suspects – like Stam, Nesta or Crespo – his lower drive evaded the attention of anyone willing to swat it away, landed on the wrong foot of Paolo Maldini and he drove the ball into the ground and past Dudek. It was 1-0 Milan with at least 89 minutes and ten seconds left to play.

As TV commentator Clive Tyldesley pointed out, only once in a Champions League Final had a trailing team turned things around, which just so happened to be the famous Manchester United revival against Bayern Munich in 1999.

Riise and Hyypiä found themselves unlucky to see their respective far volley and close header attempts denied by Milan only moments later, though it was an indication of the spirit of this Liverpool side. 'You may be better than us, but we'll always keep coming at you.' German midfielder Dietmar 'Didi' Hamann relies on this a lot when he's asked about what kept Liverpool going both in the lead-up to the match and through all of the darker times in the final itself. 'We had a great spirit,' he boasts. 'We had great togetherness, and we knew when the chips were down, we could rely on ourselves, and we trusted each other.' Judging by the coming half of football, it's a good thing they did.

The Reds kept things as boring as possible for the next ten minutes, until Milan won a corner around the 12th. Had Liverpool learned their lesson? Apparently not, but they managed to get away with it. This time, it was Seedorf who swung a chest-high ball on to the forehead of the swooping Crespo and his effort struck the same part of Luis García's body on the line.

Thus far, most of Milan's joy came from an area many wouldn't have predicted – through set pieces. But their dominance in the middle of the pitch – a feature right throughout this European campaign – was there for all to see. Gattuso constantly disrupted Liverpool's flow, Seedorf broke lines to distort the defence, Pirlo stretched his full-backs' legs as much as possible, and Kaká occasionally threatened with cute bursts of his talent. Liverpool's Harry Kewell being forced off soon after 20 minutes didn't help with addressing that midfield overload either. His replacement Vladimir Šmicer naturally preferred to be near the touchlines which left Baroš far more isolated than usual. Stam and Nesta made light work of immobilising the Czech presser, and Milan had even fewer things to worry about while Liverpool were likely counting down the seconds until they could come in at the break to receive some tactical redirection. It wouldn't surprise me if the *Rossoneri* deliberately preyed on that insecurity to see how far they could go this half to take the fixture away from the English club, which would be easily achievable should Crespo and Shevchenko get used to Benítez's high defensive line and get in behind.

Moments later, luck would desert Liverpool in more ways than one. Luis García took advantage of a rare lapse in Italian concentration to get the run on Alessandro Nesta. He chopped the ball with his right as Nesta prematurely slid in, but the ball took a fortuitous ricochet off the defender before Maldini stepped in. García led the protests as he believed the ball to have been slapped away by Nesta's hand and therefore deserving of a penalty. The referee disagreed and play continued with Kaká receiving more room than he should have with his strikers advancing ahead on either side. A chip through to Shevchenko on the right spelled trouble, before he cut the ball back to Crespo to knock it in with an off-balance swipe of his right foot. Two-nil. Liverpool had only five minutes longer to stay as strong as they could before half-time.

Unfortunately for them, Kaká was still intent on damage. He took the ball on the half-turn from

Pirlo, left Gerrard striding the other way, and freed up the space he needed to steer the ball around Carragher's slide and into Crespo. Continuing the trend, he too took it in his stride to dink it beyond Dudek and score one of the most aesthetic goals seen in a European final. 'It was one of those nights where you can do everything easily,' waxed the Argentine. 'Everything worked, every ball went where I wanted it to. It was a great feeling.'

'We were in shock,' countered Dudek. 'It was probably the most empty I've felt in my career as a football player,' revealed Hamann – and he did not arrive as a substitute until the second half.

A frantic Benítez shepherded his team into the dressing room. Once they got there, they needed direction from their manager and the Spaniard did indeed have a change in mind. But it was his assistant Alex Miller who spoke up: 'Forget about the first half,' were the first words to spread around the sullen dressing room. 'First of all you have to score as fast as you can' soon followed. Then, his 'you're Liverpool, you always play to the end' was enough to spark some energy into their captain. Gerrard formed a huddle, the players threw their arms over each other and the rallying cry began: 'Listen guys … they still believe in us. We have to give them something back.'

The trailing Reds were at least ready to go back on to the pitch with some pride to find. Meanwhile, Rafa was readying a change that he felt could throw Milan out of their rhythm, and it was a bold move. Sensing Finnan wasn't moving as he would have liked, the manager opted against a like-minded replacement to address the overrun in midfield. Dietmar Hamann was the man to replace the right-back, which shifted Riise further back to sit in front of the defence and shield them from Milan's quartet. This theoretically allowed Gerrard to venture further forward and that would hopefully enable Baroš to break the lines with Šmicer offering some pace out wide. But they would ultimately need to rely on Milan not being at their best after the break in play.

According to Crespo, there were no signs of complacency in their dressing room despite waltzing in with an overwhelming advantage. Claims of celebrating early for a game that was

The imperious presence of Silvio Berlusconi. Without him, it's impossible to predict where AC Milan would be.

Arrigo Sacchi was happy to field questions from reporters following his second European Cup win with AC Milan (v. Benfica) in 1990.

One of the greatest sides ever to represent AC Milan. Sacchi called them 'The Immortals'.

Never one to back down from a challenge, Fabio Capello assumed his full-time position as Milan head coach in the 1991/92 season.

From left to right: Frank Rijkaard, Marco van Basten and Ruud Gullit. Milan's 'Holy Trinity'.

From immortality, to invincibility. Fabio Capello's side went unbeaten in 58 games between 1991 and 1993. Fittingly, midfielder Carlo Ancelotti is central to the image.

A key figure in Capello's success, Ancelotti hung up his playing boots in 1992. The first club to offer him a coaching role was Reggiana in 1995.

Carlo points a smirk at his employer's direction, during a tumultuous period in charge of Juventus.

He returned to AC Milan as a manager in 2001, knowing that there was much work to be done.

Pictured after the UEFA Champions League Final in 2003, Paolo Maldini and Carlo Ancelotti were inseparable during their multifaceted period in Milan. Especially as this new team took shape.

Style and substance. Alessandro Nesta and Jaap Stam rarely had an opponent that could thwart them both, including Ruud van Nistelrooy.

Gattuso ran so that Pirlo could walk. And Clarence Seedorf did everything else.

Kaka cited Ancelotti's man-management as central to his development. Chats like this were regular and welcomed by the Brazilian.

A picture personifying the subjects: Andriy Shevchenko celebrating a goal and Filippo Inzaghi placed perfectly to support.

Enemies Marco Materazzi (left) and Rui Costa (right) unite for this iconic derby still.

From left to right: Serginho, Paolo Maldini, John Dahl Tomasson, Jaap Stam, Cafu, Andrea Pirlo and Rui Costa are crestfallen as the 2005 UEFA Champions League Final penalty shoot-out takes shape. Alessandro Nesta can barely watch as a routine win transforms into a nightmare.

From bad to worse. Milan are embroiled in the largest match-fixing investigation to date in 2006. The world called it 'Calciopoli' ('Footballgate')

Italy's World Cup win was a much-needed source of national pride. Massively underpinned by the best AC Milan had to offer.

Kaka's growth would reach its zenith in the wake of the Istanbul tragedy. True to form, 'Pippo' Inzaghi would be right by his side.

Same colours, different outcome. Athens was a night to remember in 2007.

The story ends the way it deserved to – with AC Milan and Carlo Ancelotti on top of the world.

Ancelotti: 'Hey Paolo, guess what?'
Maldini: 'What, boss?'
Ancelotti: 'We did it.'

already won continue to be swatted down by the fiery forward. 'Those stories are made up,' he says. 'We had players such as Alessandro Nesta, Maldini, Andrea Pirlo, Gennaro Gattuso, Clarence Seedorf, Andriy Shevchenko and many others: do you think they would celebrate after 45 minutes? Quite the opposite, there were some who were discussing how we should have been playing better, despite the fact we were beating Liverpool 3-0.'

Ancelotti was reportedly very calm at half-time and instructed many of his players to keep their heads. Their captain also rallied the troops to make sure that they would get the deal done. As Crespo explained, these were senior players. Nesta was considered the junior member of the back line at 29 years of age; Seedorf had already won the competition twice with two other teams. Many of the rest had been in the side that bettered Juventus a couple of years earlier. So, while we may want to conjure up some form of conspiracy to help explain things, we can't.

What happened next escapes mortal reasoning. It was a freak of nature.

Six minutes in Hell

A cynical foul by Sami Hyypiä on Kaká was a real turning point early into that second half. The future Ballon d'Or winner was enjoying life against the Liverpool defence and shifted the ball on the wrong side of Hyypiä before he was brought down on the edge of the area. Shevchenko did his best to make the most out of the resulting free kick, but Dudek's wall did well to close down space on his left to force him into a low drive to the right. Dudek was equal to it, but it was a wake-up call for the rest of the team. Milan were still ready to play but Liverpool now had nothing to lose.

With the ball back in play, it ricocheted to Riise who had more work to do than before to advance into the final third. He did so forcibly with Gattuso hot on his tail before he fashioned enough space in which to whip a cross into the penalty area. The ball found Steven Gerrard at the second attempt and he guided it past a scrambling Dida, before hoisting his arms into the air to cajole those travelling fans to believe that the impossible was achievable with their support.

A minute later, it was Liverpool's turn for a bit of luck when a passage of play found Milan Baroš standing in an offside position. The referee, in the spirit of maintaining the game's flow and intensity, ignored his assistant's flag as the ball meandered away from danger and out for a Liverpool throw-in. Three passes later Vladimir Šmicer launched a speculative effort from outside the area to Dida's preferred side. He should have saved it. Šmicer struck it well, and it did dip just before the line, but the goalie got a good, long, unobstructed look and should have been able to get his body behind the drive to deflect it wide of the post. Instead, he misjudged how much of the net he was covering and allowed it to skip through. 3-2. Panic stations.

Those 40,000 Liverpool fans, now in full voice, were roaring their team on every chance they got, and the noise reached deafening levels when a neat flick from Baroš released Gerrard near the penalty spot for a free shot. He was halted illegally by Gattuso, who was lucky not to be dismissed. The penalty was taken by Xabi Alonso, who forced home the rebound after Dida saved his first effort. 3-3.

The remainder of the game tells the viewer everything they need to know about either side with Liverpool's heroic, at times desperate, defending nullifying Milan's technical superiority at every turn. I hear they still talk of Djimi Traoré's goal-line clearance in hushed whispers in those Anfield shadows.

Liverpool's final change, which saw Djibril Cissé replace Milan Baroš, was a signal of their counter-attacking intent, as was Milan sticking on Jon Dahl Tomasson with five minutes of normal time to play. His best chance came in extra time as even he cursed his gangly frame for not being long enough to slide home an effort from close range. Ancelotti's side sprang forward on numerous occasions in desperate search of the strike that would surely put the rest of the contest beyond doubt but it never came. Now, with more than 127 minutes played, their fate was no longer in their hands.

The match would be decided in a penalty shoot-out.

Mark Ogden, a senior writer with ESPN, has written an insightful and compelling read on the psychology of penalty taking. He spoke to performance psychologist Tom Young, who noted the difference between the fortunes of a goalkeeper and that of a striker in this situation: 'From a keeper's perspective, penalties bring less of a threat state and more of a challenge and an opportunity to be a hero.' Why? Because penalties are expected to be scored, not saved. So, the goalkeeper usually looks good either way. Nowadays, there are data platforms and technological interventions which make things a little more difficult for the goalkeeper, such as the taker being briefed on where that goalkeeper likes to dive, and that there are more cameras available than a presidential summons to make sure their foot stays behind the line before the ball is kicked. But back then, not so much. The taker would just have to pick a side, don't change their mind, and pray that the keeper goes in the opposite direction. Or that their kick was so accurate, it couldn't be reached even if the keeper went the right way.

Young continues on a slightly poignant level: 'I remember one coach saying there is no point practising penalties as you can't replicate the pressure. They were right, of course you can't.' But there are ways a player can establish a type of penalty into their routine so as to remove most lingering doubts when it comes to appearing in grand occasions like a Champions League or World Cup Final. That said, the article ends: 'If [players] have prepared thoroughly, and followed their routine, they've done all they can do.' But even after all of that 'you can't guarantee the right result'. A number of experienced Milan stars discovered that all too painfully in Istanbul.

I'd be remiss to assume that Serginho's immediate trudge to the spot to form his run-up was a subconscious attempt to avoid Dudek unnerving him en route to Milan's maiden shot, though the mind struggles to connect his maturity with his row Z effort up and over the crossbar which handed the impetus to Liverpool. AC Milan's distress was compounded by Didi Hamann's nonchalant stroll before whipping the ball through Dida's left glove. Advantage Reds.

Pirlo took a leaf out of the German's book with an impressive strut of his own – only it can never look quite as good without the same outcome.

Outfoxed by a goalkeeper far from his line, Pirlo's lazy drive to the left found Dudek's right hand. An easy conversion from Cissé compounded his pain: 2-0 Liverpool.

A successful strike from Tomasson was barely noticed by the Milan fans, who must've suspected that the impossible was coming. But when Dida thwarted Riise's attempt at full stretch and Kaká smacked his penalty into the roof of the net to level the scoring they must have had hope. But Vladimir Šmicer was on hand to shut down optimism before it gathered any real traction. 3-2 down with one attempt remaining, Andriy Shevchenko, the man who slotted home to secure Ancelotti's revenge trophy against Juventus, ambled toward the spot knowing that a lapse of concentration would send his side home. Meanwhile, the man stopping him was ready to deploy every dirty tactic in the book if it meant he'd be on the right side of history.

Dudek's now-infamous shimmy of the hips routine on the line was apparently an homage to ex-Liverpool goalkeeper Bruce Grobbelaar from the 1984 European Cup Final. 'I didn't want to make them laugh,' he insists. 'I just wanted to put more pressure on the players.' Those Grobbelaar-esque 'spaghetti legs' were working overtime to put off the Ukrainian as he made the short run up to the penalty spot. Possibly still begrudging a late chance he had to put the game beyond doubt only to be thwarted twice at point-blank range by Dudek, apparently still an ongoing jibe between the pair, Shevchenko spent more time looking at the referee than he did the target. He did something similar against Gianluigi Buffon a couple of years earlier only now his strike was needed to keep Milan in the contest; not to win it.

He strode up confidently but it would be the angle-closing Pole who came out on top. Wiggling his way off of the goal line and into Milan's nightmares, he intercepted Shevchenko's light dink and wheeled off into the haze of disbelief that had engulfed the Atatürk stadium since the hour mark. And while Liverpool set about re-booking their celebration parade for after their flight home, a most disconcerting inquest began for the losers, which, judging by an interview with Ancelotti and UEFA in 2015, never reached a resolution.

Ten years later, that entire Istanbul affair is still 'difficult to explain' for him, though it doesn't take an expert to guess that it would have weighed heavily on a man as practical and methodical as he. Those 'six minutes of blackout' as he describes the period when Liverpool fought their way into the match were enough to 'turn the world upside down'. Since then, though he has used lessons from that day to inform crucial decisions later on in other European ventures, Ancelotti has taken a generally neutral stance on the night as a whole. Like 'it just wasn't meant to be', or 'it was one of those things', or better that it was Liverpool's 'destiny' – so as to detract the attention away from his own.

His players took a different approach in the immediate aftermath …

> 'I thought about quitting because, after Istanbul, nothing made sense anymore.'
>
> *Andrea Pirlo*

This is by far the most striking line from the masses of material woven from that day.

This is Andrea Pirlo. A man whose technical ability alone is enough to remember why the game is so beautiful and alluring in the first place. And he wanted to quit. He went on, 'The 2005 Champions League Final simply suffocated me. When that torture of a game was finished, we sat like a bunch of half-wits in the dressing room there at the stadium. We couldn't speak. We couldn't move. They'd mentally destroyed us.' On that note, it's worth remembering that the emphasis on mental health support for footballers has been a worryingly recent consideration.

Richard Heun and Alan Pringle's paper 'Football does not improve mental health: A systematic review on football and mental health disorders' explores the paradox between the science of playing the sport, and how its elite form can impact their players. Playing football (especially with your friends) can spike the levels of dopamine and serotonin in the brain as its own way of rewarding you for a job well done. Naturally, those levels decrease until your next five-a-side match and the cycle continues. Take that same activity, throw some people into the stadium and stick a poor performance on television, and the scales tip in the opposite direction – with a brutal contrast, too.

Further, they argue that the 'passion, loyalty and fanaticism that supporting a team can engender' often leads to an extreme set of behaviours by fans and players alike. In that a positive performance can induce equally positive, harmonious reactions, but that negative, 'obsessive' conduct is just as much expected if things don't go your way.

The works of like-minded scholars noted here and in other forms of modern commentary have had an indelible effect on how we understand the complex relationship between mental health and football, with organisations such as FIFPRO and the PFA now offering workshops and round-the-clock consultancy services for players in need. Back in Pirlo's day, dedicated resources on the matter were depressingly limited. The players' circle at Milan would have had enough life experience to get through most situations, though the midfielder reveals that even they weren't impervious to the comedown in 2005. 'The damage was already evident even in those early moments, and it only got more stark and serious as the hours went on.' In summary, Pirlo observes up to four disorders experienced by a number of his team-mates in the wake of that defeat: 'insomnia, rage, depression [and] a sense of nothingness'.

The sum of which was given a name: Istanbul Syndrome.

Though as much as most – outside of Liverpool – would likely sympathise with Pirlo's existential crisis, Maldini's pain after the one in eight European finals he can never forget and even Shevchenko's inability to sleep for months following the collapse, the cold embrace of reality was never too far away for any of them; nor their desperate attempts to move forward and try to forget about it.

All the wider world would have seen was a set of untouchable, pretentious big boys fallen by the industrious, plucky little guy. It resulted in a mystified appreciation of Liverpool, and a derisory gaze downward at Milan; all for a capitulation that none could have foreseen at the time, yet was as regrettable as it was entirely preventable by the people in control. Speaking of which …

CHAPTER ELEVEN

'Calciopoli'

I'M SURE you'd agree, the veil of 'properness' in football has been well and truly lifted in recent years. Especially with that 'Super League' farago, which might have ended up impacting the Italian clubs better than most.

In the 80s and 90s, Italy was the zenith of world football. It was packed full of talent. Stuart Horsfield, author of *1982 Brazil: The Glorious Failure* and senior contributor at *These Football Times* led an excerpt in the recent *Calcio II* magazine, focusing on the 1997/98 Serie A season in particular. He chose to lead with a snippet from Ronaldo, who ranked his first year with Inter high in his storied career. He called it 'tough but unforgettable', because week-in, week-out 'you'd be up against the best'. While his numbers did not match up with his phenomenal return at Barclona the season before, he credits his best development, physically and mentally, to his stay in Milan. 'I'd never seen quality like it and became a better player [for it].' He calls the Italian style a 'thinking' way of football – 'smarter' than anywhere else at the time. It's easy to understand why.

The strength of the rosters surrounding the then-World Player of the Year added provenance to his theory. Excluding the names we've already mentioned, you can add Alessandro Del Piero, Didier Deschamps, Faustino Asprilla, Roberto Ayala, Francesco Totti and Vincenzo Montella to the list of prime stars aiming to take the Scudetto championship for their own that season. Since then, it's safe to assume that Italian football has lost a large proportion of the pull on which they used to rely. They went from sitting astride the footballing world like Jupiter to standing idle and watching the rest of the game move into the new world without them. Rupert Murdoch's millions, presidential promises and fan fickleness forced Italy further down the pecking order than most could have expected before the turn of the millennium. Among these external factors sat an internal matter which threatened the integrity of the Italian game altogether; a scandal from which they are arguably still yet to recover; the visceral, unforgettable *Calciopoli* affair AKA Footballgate or *Totonero*, new and improved.

While the official origin of the title remains uncertain, its roots lay firmly in the grounds of conspiracy, sordidness and overall corruption. It's very complicated, but I'll try my best to summarise what happened. Should you wish to delve further into the issue there is a *Netflix* documentary titled *Bad Sport: Juventus*. At the heart of the controversy lies ex-Juventus managing director, Luciano Moggi, who, prior to his involvement in this scandal, led a life which would have made a Hollywood film. Sometime in the 70s Moggi had delicately networked his way from minor to major roles within various Serie A clubs, before landing in the boardroom previously held by Juventus mainstay, Italo Allodi. Both Allodi and his wannabe protege Moggi had similar upbringings, leaving mainstream education in favour of a hands-on approach to life. They immediately hit it off.

The game of football fell on to Moggi's lap as a ne'er-do-well apprentice to a Tuscan baker who moonlighted as a scout for the Italian leagues. Drawn in by the prospect of making a little extra on the side, as well as getting a first-hand look at football around the country, Moggi grasped at the opportunity to put his natural flair for negotiation and people-manipulation to the test. Jason Burke of *The Guardian* describes Moggi as a 'magnificent salesman' in an insightful exposé of the Italian magnate, in which he rightfully marvels over the man's natural nous for business and the tools he perfected over the years to take him to where he'd ultimately end up.

Burke regularly references what he calls 'the Moggi system', which followed a 'what goes around, comes around, you scratch my back, I scratch yours, once a friend always a friend' routine. It was a simple formula which, over time, perfected the art of networking.

Now, we have LinkedIn and life coaches on TikTok telling us we'd be stiffed without it, but back then, you actually had to go out and speak to people.

Over time, Moggi impressed a number of senior officials on his scouting journeys throughout the country before leaving a critical impression on Allodi in the mid-70s. So enchanted was Allodi by this slick official from the midlands that he offered an aspiring Moggi a key administrative role across Juve's scouting network once he earned a few stripes elsewhere in the league with Roma and Torino. Soon, the two struck up a friendly partnership, with Moggi licensed to see where he'd be able to take his new role for the benefit of his employers, who were keen to displace the pretenders that had taken over their *Scudetti* birthright in recent years. They were banking on 'Lucky' Luciano's shamelessness to take them to higher ground.

The mid-to-late 70s proved essential in solidifying Moggi's influence in both the football and political spectrum of the country, and his influence grew when he moved to the capital in 1975. There the velvet-tongued Italian had direct access to some senior officials of the country to build a catalogue of elite contacts. It's uncertain how soon he put them to use, but it's impossible to quantify how useful they would prove to be. Got a speeding ticket? Just phone the mayor, allegedly. Accidentally stole an item from the store? Give the owner a bell, he'll probably let you keep it, allegedly. Running a football club and want to give your team the best chance of winning? Choose the ref. Less allegedly.

For the sake of balance, I thought it best to find a few positives about Moggi. But I found something else. It's called – and I wish I was kidding – 'Sexygate', a title coined during his time with Torino when he was alleged to have arranged some 'sexy time' for a number of refereeing officials in exchange for favourable decisions. However, after a short investigation, the Turin magistrates acquitted him of 'favouring prostitution and sports fraud' for his own personal gain. Which is why I suspect it seldom came up in his talks with Allodi years later. Less hypothetical though, would be an assessment of the landscape of Italian football and how that would feed into the infamy that came later on.

Just as much as football has always been the most celebrated sport in the country, Italy has, and may always have, a corrupt culture which sullies the reputation of *calcio* beyond repair. This has been cultivated by those looking to harness the influence of the game and its all-consuming nature to feed their own power-trip. Thus they slowly chip away at its integrity and plunge its morality deeper into the void. John Foot's *Calcio* proudly recites the work of Gigi Garanzini's pioneering *They still call it Calcio, in* which he argues that Italian football has been 'genetically modified' through time – much like its wider society – to resemble an imitation that 'had grown rich far too quickly, leaving its values behind in a rush to earn, spend and pollute' everything that once made it great. Over time, Moggi developed into the archetype of the vision Garanzini wishes he had not predicted.

Moggi's biographer, Marco Travaglio, records how his subject 'understood the value of media and advertising very early on', and that the 'soul of the business' (this being the match result) was central to everything else. Juventus formed a foundation strong and stable enough to benefit from this footballing strategy. Typically, Moggi found allies there, too, beginning with the Agnelli family. Presiding over the club since 1923 and owning the FIAT car company for even longer, their expanding business portfolio funnelled into a 90s economic renovation for Juventus until Lazio and Milan scrabbled at their perch. Juve appointed Moggi in 1994 as their new sporting director, sandwiching him into a direct support line with president Antonio Giraudo and ex-player Roberto Bettega. Together, they became the *triade*, one of Italian football's most infamous, yet effective, business trios. Add in Moggi's agent son Alessandro and his significance to a wider GEA agency group and you had everything you needed to build another great Juventus team. One with Pavel Nedvěd, David Trezeguet, Lilian Thuram and many of their friends.

With everything in place, Juventus laid waste to the Italian league. They toppled Milan to take home both *Scudetti* 2005 and 2006 in what looked like an 'all's fair in love and war' situation with the Turin powerhouse peaking on top of that Italian mountain. The club's board had once even marvelled that the so-called *triade* had 'fashioned a sober and above all winning model of management'.

Almost like an example that ought to be followed by others who wanted to replicate their success.

Few had suspected that possibly the younger Moggi's influence as an agent was questionable, but GEA's proud understanding of the Bosman invention and the lack of governance for representation in football as a whole worked against any substantiated claims. Daddy Moggi, too, was revered. Football journalist Giancarlo Galavotti argued that he 'should be considered as a sort of godfather of Italian football' and a 'ruler of the transfer market' given the energy he committed to his craft. At his best, he was believed to be making somewhere between 400 and 500 telephone calls per day. Suppose he needed to contact the *triade* to work through their next move: 'Sunday night at mine, lads – I'll put the kettle on!' Or that there was a footballer who needed seducing to play for Juve the next season: 'How about I fly you and your family out here so you can take a look? Great, I'll send the jet!' Or suppose he was concerned about the status of the refereeing in matches and felt like he needed to have his voice heard: 'He has to be stopped. Both the assistants too!' Be sure to note which one is the actual quote here, by the way ...

In May 2006, what started out as an investigation into the *Camorra* (the name for the Neapolitan version of the Mafia) for illegal match betting a couple of years before, revealed a broken footballing system with Moggi sitting prettily at the peak of 'a cupola of power marked by alliances between the managers of some big clubs, agents and referees'. After that the authorities kept a close eye on 'Lucky' Luciano's movements, tapping his phones and transcribing conversations in search for illicit activity.

By the middle of the month, a large number of referees had either been fired or were coerced to resign from Italian football. Franco Carraro and Tullio Lanese, the president, of the Football Federation and the Referees' Association respectively, moved out as the heat increased. Each was believed to have been under Moggi's influence when distributing 'favourable' referees to Juve games and 'understanding' officials to their rivals'. Even a presenter of a well-known football chat show, Aldo Biscardi, was removed from his post for apparently helping with Moggi's post-game image if certain decisions revealed an element of bias.

Juve's 29th championship win on 14 May did little to deflect the hammer that was about to strike Moggi's operation. More names came forward, further inquiries were called, and the wake of the scandal was as palpable as it was startlingly quick to reach its conclusion. In summary, sociologist Marco Revelli wrote a counter-statement to the one provided by Juve's board earlier on in this chapter: 'The ethical and aesthetic catastrophe of the triade reflects the anthropological degeneration of contemporary Italy.' Naturally, the main perpetrator took umbrage at this and other slights were aimed in his direction.

> 'Being portrayed as a thief was really painful. I felt really beaten down, like an entire house had crashed on top of me … it's as if I was at the top of a tree and everyone below was taking aim, ready to take shots at me.'
>
> *Luciano Moggi*

Moggi's personal plight aside, the consequences of *Calciopoli* (or *'Moggiopoli'*) were nothing short of devastating for the welfare and reputation of *calcio* en masse.

Once the courts had enough time to reflect on the masses of material presented by the prosecution, the Court of Cassation – Italy's Supreme Court – ruled that while Moggi was an obvious target, he couldn't have acted on his own, concluding that he was heading 'a significantly structured association widely diffused across the whole territory with every single person involved fully aware [of what was going on].' But as the 'head' of this unofficial organisation, he attracted most of the attention.

As a result, Juventus were robbed of some of their greater on-field assets, who left for pastures new abroad and away from the shame of Serie A. Fabio Cannavaro and Emerson followed manager Fabio Capello out of the door to Real Madrid, while Gianluca Zambrotta and Lilian Thuram teamed up on enemy turf in Barcelona. Zlatan Ibrahimovic and Patrick Vieira formed another pair of ex-Turin stars leaving the club the summer following the scandal, but stayed closer to home with Inter, one of the few big domestic teams that escaped the gaze of the bloodthirsty magistrates, much to the dismay of Moggi who scorned the lack of depth in the investigation.

The now-disgraced sporting director concedes – through gritted teeth – that 'if I make a mistake, I pay the consequences' when referring to his exile from the Italian game. He did, however, manage to escape jail time through the statute of limitations expiring ten years after the initial conspiracy was brought to the authorities' attention. But even that's not enough to remove his bitterness. 'They said Juventus were winning because Moggi was helping Juventus,' which he somehow believes 'is not true', insisting it was more to do with his abilities as a director than anything untoward. Also, that 'for *Calciopoli* to exist, they should have considered all the clubs, because football has to be watched at 360 degrees, not only considering one club and excluding all the others'.

In fairness, if anybody were to know who else to blame, it should be him. After all, it was his network through which the scandal was largely able to worm its way through those two seasons (at least), and a few of the thousands of transcripts pulled from his phone records reveal that other big clubs had taken a slice out of that Juve pie, despite Silvio Berlusconi's weirdly transparent claims to the contrary.

Shamelessly, in the face of the allegations, Milan's leader regularly denied his closeness with Moggi, with Galliani close by to back each move. At the time, Berlusconi's right hand was reportedly incensed at the idea that his Milano family would become voluntarily embroiled in such sordid activity, as it played directly against the fabric of the club and how they'd conducted themselves during his tenure. When the news broke, he scolded reporters who suggested otherwise: 'It's clear even to a child that Turin is attempting, through its political and sporting newspapers and lawyers, to involve Milan in order to ease its own position.' He also insisted that Milan's system was 'not the same' as Juve's – whatever that means.

It can hardly be denied that Moggi was not the only perpetrator in the saga, nor that Galliani or Berlusconi were just poor fall guys for their old mate's indiscretions. But the law's response must be respected. Several clubs were found to have been involved in *Calciopoli* and thus faced retribution. In no particular order, and after a lengthy appeal procedure, the final indictment reads as follows:

- Reggiana were docked 11 points and fined €100,000
- Lazio were docked three points and banned from that year's UEFA Cup
- Fiorentina started the season 15 points behind and with no UCL football
- Milan lost eight points as well as 30 from the previous year
- Juventus were relegated to Serie B, started with nine points fewer than the rest of their new league and were stripped of their two titles since the start of the investigation

Milan probably felt their pinch lightest of all. It was a win for Berlusconi, who'd escaped the Moggi attention by the skin of his teeth. The pair had allegedly met on a number of occasions, including at Berlusconi's home in the early 2000s, to see if Luciano could get 'lucky' in Milan, though an official bid was never lodged in his direction. It was an untypically timid approach from the brash Italian owner who was used to getting what he wanted.

Nevertheless, Moggi went away and Milan returned to the Milanello Sports Centre that summer dazed and confused. Remember, not a single player was indicted by the scandal, nor were any found to have been involved in any wrongdoing. Yet they were tarred with the same brush that had painted a division everybody believed was corrupt. It was a tough gig for the foreign players who were not accustomed to how things worked in this unfamiliar part of the world, and tougher still for the local lads who were aiming to focus on their group trip to Germany rather than pay much attention to things back home.

On reflection the 2006 World Cup in Germany must go down as one of the more memorable international tournaments of the modern era. And it ended spectacularly with Italy, reeling from scandal, beating France with Zinedine Zidane disfiguring his final match by being sent off for headbutting Marco Materazzi.

But not even the glittering World Cup trophy could blind the authorities from the task at hand. The 2006/07 season started in September with Carlo Ancelotti's men eight points behind the pack before a ball had even been kicked.

CHAPTER TWELVE

'Damage Control'

HAD HE had things entirely his own way in the wake of *Calciopoli*, I don't think Ancelotti would have wanted to make too many reinforcements that summer. The team had a really nice balance between attack and defence, and it was difficult to locate a definite hole which needed filling in the transfer market. Milan finished second only to Juventus before the authorities knocked on their door and they had a far superior goal difference. But perhaps they had a lack of pragmatism to salvage the single point if three were still on offer plus the controversy was mixed with Father Time.

Jaap Stam was 34 years old at the start of the season and was clearly struggling for the pace he put so well to use during his youth. The proud

Dutchman had also admitted to feeling 'homesick' early in the previous season, and had hoped for a move in the January. But he stayed faithful to his original request to leave by the end of the 2005/06 season and the manager duly obliged. From his perspective, Father Time's work made for a wiser head than most, though experience and exemplary match behaviour was one thing Ancelotti had in abundance in his first team squad. All in all, Stam would represent a fair deal for Ajax at around £2.5m – less than a third of the investment Milan mande to sign him for themselves – with the then-technical director describing the veteran as 'a great asset to our young and talented team'. Unfortunately Stam would spend only a single season there before retiring in October 2007.

Another heartfelt loss came when Rui Costa's own home called his name. A year older than Jaap and with an emerging Kaká at the forefront of Carlo's plans, the inevitable was as near as it was clear. Fittingly, it would be his beloved Benfica fulfil the dream of the boy who wanted a return 'since the day [he] left the club' in 1994. As with Stam, the club had registered their interest in bringing him home earlier in the season, but Costa stayed loyal to his Milan commitments until the summer, whereupon a Bosman-induced return to Portugal was secured not long before he could thank everyone who helped to carve out his *trequartista* image. Fifteen years later, Costa was sworn in as Benfica's 34th president, with more than 84 per cent of the votes leaning in his favour.

Milan seemed to have gotten off lightly post-*Calciopoli* damages. But there was much worse to come, and in very confusing circumstances.

> 'It has been a bitter summer, because the credibility of football in general and Milan in particular have been called into question. As captain I feel I have lost something over the last two years … but you cannot accuse him of being a traitor, and we will always be grateful for what Sheva has given us.'
>
> *Paolo Maldini on Shevchenko leaving Milan*
> *in 2006*

Transfers are a seriously misunderstood, yet enormously powerful factor in modern football. Ideally, you have a player who wants to move to a certain club; those wishes are reciprocated by a side possessing the resources required to structure a deal. But that's what's seen on the surface. Daniel Geey, an accomplished sports lawyer and author of *Done Deal: An Insider's Guide to Football Contracts, Multi-Million Pound Transfers and Premier League Big Business*, briefly assessed the 'complicated' reality of player moves in a 2019 article for *GQ* titled 'What really goes on behind the scenes of a big football transfer'. The simple answer being: a lot. Beginning with that initial interest which can become 'a game of interlinked negotiations', where 'the club's directors, technical team, scouts and manager need a very clear picture of what the team's budget will be' before pinpointing the target that best fits their needs. Then, with everybody on the same page, it should be down to the players themselves to fulfil the wishes of their new employer, having agreed on what their remit would be prior to joining. But for reasons that became clearer in the years following Andriy Shevchenko's record-breaking move to Chelsea in 2006, this particular swoop was doomed to disappoint before the ink was dry.

That same Chelsea train that picked up Crespo three years earlier, had apparently been tracking the Ukrainian's movements for just as long. A number of insiders within the club had earmarked the likes of Samuel Eto'o and Carlos Tevez on their hunt for a top-class striker to fit owner Roman Abramovich's mission statement. Crespo did not do too badly, Mateja Kežman barely did anything at all, and Adrian Mutu did even less than that before Didier Drogba showed them all how it was done. Manager José Mourinho took the uncommon decision to deploy Drogba as his number one forward without an additional striker beside him, immediately plunging secondary forwards into the role of an understudy in case the Ivorian was injured or less important matches required a rotation.

So for Mourinho, a manager who had tried to incorporate multiple big-name strikers into the team only to be dissatisfied with them, it was important that if he were to be 'forced' to sign another one, that they either dovetailed with Drogba or was similar to him yet happy to play that secondary role. I cannot believe that would

258

satisfy the 2004 Ballon d'Or winner fresh from scoring 175 goals in 296 games for one of the best clubs of his generation. Neither would that be the owner's intention when he signed a £30 million cheque for his services. It was a classic case of owner and manager not being on the same page, with an off-pace, disheartened Andriy Shevchenko left unawares and isolated.

Drogba and Mourinho was a professional bromance for the ages, with the Ivorian target man ever present during his first two years at Stamford Bridge, and largely responsible for the two Premier League titles that Chelsea won.

Despite this, murmurs grew progressively louder at the higher end of the club with the board unsure of how they were going to function in the long term with only one world-class 'target man'. So, before that could become an issue, they took matters into their own hands.

A natural networker, Abramovich's burgeoning book of contacts revealed a series of numbers belonging to representatives close to the Ukrainian who he'd been tracking ever since taking over. Words were exchanged, agreements were made, and Chelsea shirts with 'Shevchenko 7' on the back were being printed quicker than you could say 'Didier, I can explain'. Then again, Mourinho didn't have to.

The lion's share of his selection and tactical focus remained on the Ivorian sensation, with his relationship with the Chelsea hierarchy deteriorating as a result. He would be unceremoniously dismissed the following season, but not before his glitzy Ukrainian present had lost his patience. Unlike Stam and Costa who made sensible moves to preserve their legacy, Shevchenko was led right into the firing line by a promise which could never be fulfilled. That didn't stop the UK press from picking up on the easier story of a 'once great striker failing the Premier League test', and he's been rendered a categorical transfer 'flop' ever since.

Despite insisting that his decision to leave Milan for Chelsea 'wasn't a mistake', his time in London stands as one of the most extraordinarily unsuccessful deals in terms of its payment-to-returns ratio for Chelsea. It's a label he doesn't deserve and one that would not have happened had common sense overruled ego. Adriano Galliani has never hidden his regret over the Shevchenko sale, and believes he would have blasted through some of those Serie A scoring records had he found a way to block it.

But while the Chelsea hierarchy had the first-world headache of trying to enjoy whatever bit of magic they could eke out of this awkward situation with Sheva, Galliani and Milan had the unenviable task of having to endure life without him.

Even with a hefty chunk of the transfer window remaining, it didn't take a genius to appreciate how big of a hole his sale would leave in the squad, and that it would probably take more than one body to fill it given the situation in which Milan found themselves at the beginning of the season. Referee speculation, point deductions, lesser chance of European football. None of this was conducive to finding a like-for-like replacement for one of the best strikers of all time.

Their first stop on the tour to solve the unsolvable came in the form of misfiring Real Betis striker Ricardo Oliveira, who'd had a fairly unremarkable career for a striker who emerged during a rusty era for Brazilian forwards. Milan signed the *Seleção* international for not too far off of €20 million. Unfortunately, this would be a precursor of how the Milanese giants would conduct themselves on a number of occasions moving forward, particularly when it came to addressing their striking issue. Similarly, would Oliveira relish challenges less strenuous than being the San Siro's focal point? He made a loan move to La Liga's Zaragoza for the second season of his two-year employment in Italy and averaged a goal every other game during that season in Spain. But in Milan, he had managed one every eight. It cannot have been easy for him as in the October his sister, Maria Lourdes, was kidnapped. She was released unharmed on 12 March 2007.

The other frontman signing needs no introduction. He doesn't even need a forename. It was Ronaldo. Not Cristiano, obviously. It was the 'real one' as some like calling him. He waltzed through the San Siro doors with a legacy painting him as one of the most naturally gifted strikers in football history. The balance, the power, the focus. At his peak he was a true phenomenon. And at 30 years of age he arguably still had a good couple of years left in the tank at the elite level. In truth, he arrived at Milan as a more well-rounded striker; just but not how they would have liked. Even his arrival was unnecessarily complicated.

Tasting some of the medicine used to stall the Stam and Costa departures the season before, Milan themselves were made to wait longer than anticipated to secure Ronaldo from Real Madrid. Ironically, the biggest hurdle was laid by Fabio Capello, who had embarked on a second spell at the Bernabéu in a bid to overturn their dry spell. Instead, he reportedly feuded with a number of Madrid players who took offence to his pragmatism in attack, namely Antonio Cassano and Ronaldo. This friction wouldn't be immediate, it could only grow over time, and beyond the barriers of the summer transfer window, by which point Milan had little option but to bite their tongue until the winter trading period offered them a chance to go back in for the Brazilian. By this point, *Los Blancos* were happy to accept the meagre €7.5 million offered by an opportunistic Galliani, who punctuated his excitement by describing this as a 'very satisfactory agreement for a top-class player' to the horde of reporters congregated in Milan for his unveiling. An emotionless Capello simply wished him safe travels on his way out the training ground, while Ronaldo offered a franker explanation for why he chose to leave the club for which he had such admiration: 'I never had any problems with the coach,' he said, 'but he didn't want me.' The speculation focused on Ronaldo's fitness, his willingness to acquiesce to Capello's strict regimen as the source of the pair's issues, and even Ancelotti offers little by way of counsel in the striker's corner to argue otherwise. Ancelotti admitted that Ronaldo was 'not particularly fit' when they met for contract discussions, but maintained that he was still 'a great player [who] brings a lot of enthusiasm to the team'.

Continuing this disappointing trend, once Ronaldo was officially unveiled on 18 January, he was almost unrecognisable, not just for the holiday weight which he took to Italy, but for the number he was given on arrival. His association with the number 9 shirt was undeniable, yet it was impossible with Milan having put that egg in Oliveira's basket.

As a compromise, Milan printed the same number twice, but I suspect not too many 'Ronaldo 99' jerseys left the megastore that season. Certainly not as many as the typical 'Ronaldo 9' versions displayed in the Madrid stores during their *Galactico* marketing campaign. But not to worry, if 99 was to be the sum of the problems Ronaldo would have in Milan, the Champions League wasn't one. He was prohibited from playing in the competition for the rest of the 2006/07 campaign by UEFA having already represented Real Madrid in the group.

Starting off the season with an eight-point deduction, Milan lacked any real impetus to take each game to their opposition in the hope of finding some momentum to be dominant in this league campaign. They approached most like a grand National prospect with a clipped hoof; almost tentatively going into matches knowing of what they're capable but unsure of whether or not to tighten the screw if it meant dropping further from the herd for the same reason they'd trailed Juventus in 2005/06.

Perhaps opting to focus on the technical side of their game with the ball on the deck, knowing that they no longer possessed a cold-blooded finisher who could be relied upon to take most of the chances they could make, there was a clearly more stable, sensible and arrogant way of moving the ball around in midfield. It was a domestic year in which Pirlo really came into his own, while Seedorf made a slight change from an all-conquering, box-to-box midfielder to a more cultured advanced playmaker on either side of the midfield behind the dedicated *trequartista*. Plus, it was a time when they saw the best from long-term squad man Massimo Ambrosini, a man whose modesty tends to cover up the acclaim his endeavour deserves.

Massimo was a 'quiet leader'. A player who led by example, the type of man whose face would not adorn the posters on the bedroom walls of most aspiring youngsters, but who would most certainly hear about him they were under the right coaching guidance. Watching him would teach youngsters that football is not a game of individuals but a team sport which requires the vanity of certain players to be sidelined to help the collective. Some may use the same description for Gattuso for reasons we can all understand. But they had different ways of remaining where they stood.

Gattuso would snarl, almost to frighten you into submission and scythe you down if you dared to ignore that early warning. Ambrosini would keep a mental note of any time he thought you stepped out of line and let his decisions on the ball do the talking, planting that seed of doubt in an opponent's mind should they dare think to challenge him again. Gattuso would make the headlines, Ambrosini might make the footer. It's also worth remembering that in those darker periods of big-name departures from Milan, Ambro remained. 'Those days were emotionally very hard,' he reflected. 'We understood that we would lose a pillar of that team there.' Yet despite feeling 'the fear of remaining in a situation that would no longer be what it was before', the velvet-haired midfielder's service to *I Rossoneri* ended after 18 years in 2013. I was there to watch his unmistakably vibrant frame swagger up the red carpet onto the San Siro turf for their 120th year anniversary a couple of years ago, and I suspect every fan in attendance appreciated the opportunity to thank him once again.

Moreover, Ambrosini wasn't the only fringe player to start having a real influence on AC Milan this season. The credit Ambro deserves should be equally shared among Marek Jankulovski, Alberto Gilardino, Yoan Gourcuff, Dario Šimić and Cristian Brocchi among others. 'Magic' Marek's special value came by virtue of his extreme versatility. Also topping the rest of the aforementioned group by way of Serie A experience, Milan knew what they were getting when they had purchased Jankulovski from Udinese for an undisclosed fee back in 2005. A consistent professional, he would help increase their dwindling numbers in the full-back areas.

Tellingly, his arrival came only a few days following the Istanbul nightmare. The speed with which Carlo acted to draft in an additional left-back reveals a couple of things. Namely, that perhaps a bit of cold-hearted logic wouldn't go amiss in future to avoid future collapses, and that maybe it was time to begin thinking of life without

Paolo Maldini in that position, even if the man himself had other plans.

Maldini's earlier career revolved around his natural flair for adaptation. One might argue that the esteem with which we handle his name wouldn't be needed if it were not for his early relocation from winger to left-back. Others could go one further to use that same idea in relation to changing positions again at nearly 40 years of age. This time he moved from left-back to centre-back. Looking back at the change, Maldini remembers those inaugural principles instilled by Arrigo Sacchi: 'In the Sacchi years, we were guided by this idea of the game, the full-back had to follow certain indications without his characteristics, not allowing the man to pass.' Bu this was not a stone-wall principle, and instead depending on 'the needs' of the team at any given time. 'Some profiles can adapt, others are more limited,' opined the legendary *Milanisti*. 'You have to have some flexibility.' So he proved by prolonging his already exceptional playing career by a further three years at centre-back; without the strains of getting up and down the touchline. Ancelotti marvels at the exemplary behaviour of his captain, insisting 'players like him give confidence to the whole team'. As did Cafu, who described his team-mate as 'an inspiration', not just for him, 'but for all players who are 30 and think they can't play anymore'. However, without the option of moving infield, the next couple of seasons saw Cafu's involvement fall away.

As the saying goes, 'all good things must come to an end'. Even a career as captivating and exemplary as the great Cafu's.

Andrea Pirlo said that he was 'trend-setting in being one of the first truly great attacking full-backs. Excellent at getting forward, but very strong defensively as well.' Andriy Shevchenko described him as 'a warrior on the field and a sincere, kind man off it. Strong and powerful, his runs from defence led to numerous goals at AC Milan and his jokes helped to ease the pressure during training and in matches.' Then there's Jaap Stam. A man of few words, but not in this case: 'He's the type of full-back we like in Holland, who likes to take the initiative to attack, but also comes back as quick as he can to defend. He's a great person as well. He's played for the national team, won trophies for the national team, and he's been outstanding for years and years. People tend to forget that defensively he was very strong, but he stands out because of his attacking impulses and energy. Cafu just kept going – up and down, up and down – and never gave up.'

He was a World Cup star, a Champions League ambassador, a Serie A game-changer, a Soccer Aid merchant. The man did it all. His boots appeared an impossibly large and daunting pair to fill, and it comes as no surprise that it took more than one player to do it. Much like the Shevchenko omission, only Cafu's solution stayed in-house. Nevertheless, Giuseppe Favalli and later Massimo Oddo did exceptionally well in the circumstances.

Alberto Gilardino, transferred from Parma in 2005, was unfortunate to be born in an era of truly blessed Italian forwards, but he was able to come into his own at times in 2006/07. Fleetingly and in intermittent periods, perhaps, but goals are goals especially in the UEFA Champions League.

Neither the tallest nor the most powerful, Gilardino was nevertheless a very progressive forward player. Good at tracking defenders' movement and anticipating where some space might develop, he became one of their main forwards in the immediate aftermath of the Istanbul season – scoring regularly to earn a spot in the Italian World Cup setup. He wasn't a regular starter at the tournament, but a goal to equal the one scored by the United States is well recognised by the *Azzurri* faithful. The pair have held a professional fondness stemming back nearly 20 years since 2004, when he turned out for the Italian Olympic squad and was crowned as UEFA's 'Golden Boy' for a standout role in the Azzurrini's UEFA U21 EURO Championship winning team.

Things appeared slightly different under Carlo Ancelotti; a man Gilardino has described as 'exceptional, in terms of technical value of mentality'. The same man who didn't see his latest purchase ready enough to disrupt his preferred lineup with Shevchenko leading most of the way, but the new season was a very different opportunity for the nomadic forward.

He wore Milan colours a further 40-odd times this year, but the team as a whole suffered with the instability caused through the variety of

changes at the top of Ancelotti's 'Christmas Tree'.
Losing Shevchenko was one thing, but forcing the
Oliveira peg into the Milanese hole was another.
Plus, flirting with Ronaldo on the side was never
going to do much for team morale or overall
consistency in scoring. Part of why the prior squads
had been such a success was the allowance of time
and practice to fashion Ancelotti's favoured squad
into his favourite formation. It was a theme which
stretched right across his elite achievement of
winning four European Cups, more than any other
manager and a raft of domestic championships.

Asking the man to compose a 'dream team' of
his best 11 players was tough, but when he did face
up to it, he answered with a selection from five of
his former clubs: Parma, Juventus and AC Milan as
well as Chelsea and Paris Saint-Germain – whom
he joined after leaving Milan in 2009. Eleven years
on, five of those are players he met during this
book's timeline: Cafu, Paolo Maldini, Andrea
Pirlo, Kaká and Andriy Shevchenko. Naturally,
fans were incensed at a number of omissions.
Namely, Alessandro Nesta and Clarence Seedorf,
though preferring John Terry and Frank Lampard

helps to explain his thinking. The manager did offer some solace in a 2020 interview with BT with regards to how important the Dutch midfielder was in the bigger moments. He calls Seedorf a player with 'strong character, strong personality and it was impossible for him to miss a top game'. But then it would be easier for him to miss a less significant match if it preserved his energy for when the team needed it most. Understanding his players, making sure they understood their roles and enjoying the consistency it creates was what made Ancelotti one of the game's very best man-managers. But wading through the mud to find out which tree grew the highest was just as important. Even if it meant trying a variety of techniques that work against domestic form.

Oliveira, despite being 'delighted to sign for a big club like Milan', found himself crippled by both circumstance and expectation. Ironically, though his form in La Liga with Real Betis had both caught Milan's eye and granted Betis passage to the UEFA Champions League, a knee ligament injury sustained in that very competition would come to plague him in Italy, resulting in a frustrating season which began in its latter half, and resulted in fewer goals than one hand could count. Ronaldo did better, scoring two while assisting another on his debut, before going on to average one in two until the end of his first season. But as he was barred from playing in Europe, that burden largely fell on Gilardino. Gilardino didn't do that well in the competition either, though he did follow up on a tough, goalless campaign the season before with two goals this time around.

> 'I think that we didn't deserve to lose in 2005, and I think it was destiny that gave us the opportunity to replay. I was sure that we were going to win in 2007.'
>
> *Carlo Ancelotti reflecting on the 2006/07*
> *Champions League campaign*

CHAPTER THIRTEEN

'The Road to Redemption'

'WHO COULD have imagined it?' begins the AC Milan website's recap of the 2006/07 European campaign. Choosing to address the *Calciopoli* elephant in the room and the reduced preparation time for the season ahead, most foresaw a difficult time for Milan in the tournament even though it was not affected by their domestic points deduction, but which now required an enforced entrance match against Red Star Belgrade. A tough task made a lot easier by Filippo Inzaghi.

Although signed by Fatih Terim in time for the 2001/02 season, 'Pippo' would find his spiritual home in Milan under Ancelotti. Like his manager, Inzaghi rose to the Juve peak before individualism struck. Searching for a squad in need of his very specific 'find me and I'll score' mindset, he was lured in by the prospect of having Shevchenko as his partner and Rui Costa as their source. Though his place in the squad was by no means guaranteed, and a few months of instability was to come before Ancelotti settled things down, his 42 per cent European conversion rate at Juventus would come in handy should Milan learn how to harness his ability, even if it meant bending to the whim of one of world football's most polarising strikers.

I've seldom come across strikers who divide opinion as much as Inzaghi. Among his dissenters sit two men from the very zenith of world football: Sir Alex Ferguson and Johan Cruyff. Ferguson's comical 'the lad must've been born offside' quip dilutes Cruyff's more damning conclusion that Inzaghi actually couldn't play football, and was just 'always in the right position'. Then you have Pippo's compatriot Vincenzo Montella, who said, 'Even today I can't explain how he managed to score so many goals. He couldn't dribble, he couldn't shoot from outside the box [and] had half the talent of players who had half the success.' Perhaps Cruyff's assessment explains why that is.

Inzaghi wasn't the type of player to take the game by the scruff of the neck and force the play in the right direction with the ball at his feet. I doubt he was capable of doing that in a league like Serie A anyway. The obstinate nature of defending in that part of the world wouldn't accept anything but overwhelming confidence and conviction in a striker's approach to scoring goals. But instead of getting stuck in his own incompetence, he sharpened his few tools to become one of the game's ultimate poachers, a role ideally suited to his supreme footballing intelligence, naturally opportunistic thought process and shameless desire to score goals above anything else. He was probably not the type of player to rely on if you were looking to him to unlock defences on his own, but he was more than capable of popping up in situations few could predict. Much like the uncompromising two-legged tie against a driven and physically fitter Red Star Belgrade side hell-bent on piling misery on Ancelotti's hapless, disgraced AC Milan team.

'Our opponents have been training for two months and have already started their national league,' said Inzaghi days before the first leg.

'But we will do our best, we know why we are here, but we now have the chance to earn a place in the next stage of the Champions League and this means a lot to us.' Ancelotti certainly was not taking any chances, and fielded an impressive line-up for the first leg at the San Siro. Inzaghi duly obliged following typically free-flowing work by Kaká to slide home after a move in the 20th minute. In the second leg, Gennaro Gattuso would be the provider for Inzaghi, who converted a close-range header to put the tie further beyond Red Star, before a brutish effort from Clarence Seedorf established a 3-0 aggregate in favour of Milan. Moments later Red Star gave their home support something to celebrate with a consolation goal, but Ancelotti's men marshalled the rest of the game well and had their sights set firmly on the group stage. Mercifully dodging any of the top performers, Milan were drawn in Group E alongside Lille, AEK Athens and Anderlecht. It started in ideal fashion on a mid-September evening which pitted Milan at home against arguably the group's weakest team, AEK Athens. The Greek side rolled over as Milan strolled to a 3-0 win, with a Gourcuff strike sandwiched between an Inzaghi opener and Kaká penalty. A goalless match against Lille was alleviated by results and it was left to Kaká to keep his team on top the group. The elegant Brazilian followed up on a crucial winner away at Anderlecht in October, with a hat-trick to sink the Belgians at the San Siro at the beginning of November. His San Siro spectacle drew plaudits from all over, including within his own dressing room, not least from a gushing Ancelotti who was all too proud to make up for Kaká's humility. 'He's exceptional. He can do absolutely anything,' his delighted manager said after the second Anderlecht match. 'For me, he's the best player in the world at the moment.'

Even losing their final two matches was not enough to remove them from top spot with ten points. By this point, their blueprint for the tournament had been established even if some of the squad was growing old. It was necessary for Ancelotti to place the elder statesmen with the younger ones. It was also Ancelotti's responsibility to build a stem in the 4-3-2 section of his

'Christmas Tree' formation with Inzaghi the star on the top. And he had to position Kaká where he could soar to greater heights without letting his wings burn. These were three elements that would prove critical as his side ventured through a gruelling Champions League examination littered with challenges each more complicated than the last. It began with a round of 16 fixture against Celtic.

With the newer formations of UEFA's cup competitions, it's tough luck on Celtic that their prior efforts aren't as praised as they deserve to be. Celtic have a richer history than most in the European Cup. They became European champions directly the summer after England conquered the world in 1966, though unlike their geographical relatives, there's no mistaking the 'rightful' owners of their title. Clearly legitimate goals by two Tommy Gemmell and Stevie Chalmers confirmed a successful 2-1 victory over Inter Milan at a packed-out Estadio Nacional in Lisbon. In doing so, they claimed the Scottish giants' one and only top European honour in their history, but added it to a mind-boggling quintuple achievement.

They pipped their Glaswegian rivals Rangers to the league title by three points, and claimed both the Scottish Cup and Scottish League Cup with ease. Then they captured the Glasgow Cup to banish any doubt of their dominance that year. Five titles, one season, a feat yet to be matched by a British club.

Central to it all was the legendary Jock Stein, one third of a managerial triumvirate forever immortalised in Jonny Owens' *The Three Kings*, an incredible story of a friendship ensconced within a fierce rivalry between the United Kingdom's three best clubs. The other two members – Manchester United's Sir Matt Busby and Liverpool's Bill Shankly – were liberal in confessing their admiration for Stein, and were believed to have frequently visited his neck of the woods in the off-season to talk shop and let the evening wind down. Poignantly, Owens chooses Stein when pressed to pick who was the most impressive. Not only does he describe Stein's legacy as 'nothing short of remarkable' but he also noted that he was 'the greatest domestic football manager that has ever lived'. His success and football ethos is embedded into the fabric of Celtic Football Club; the belief that while it may be important to win a match, the manner in which you win is 'even more important' has never left them. Nor has his will to succeed for the fans' benefit above any personal gain. It's a motto which remains even after Stein's death in 1985, and is an intangible driver pushing every modern Celtic side to their limits – even if their recent involvement in Europe's most coveted prize appears more like a privilege than a certainty. Milan experienced this dogged persona first-hand.

The pair had met in the group stages of the 2004/05 campaign, and that 3-1 Milan win was the largest deficit in this fixture's history in Europe. Even then it came courtesy of two late goals. At home that year, despite there being no chance of progressing, Celtic ground out a 0-0 shutout. They kept much of that stubbornness in this first leg in 2007 – which ended with an identical scoreline after a fairly even contest in front of a vibrant Celtic Park.

Contrary to general assumption, their manager Gordon Strachan was aiming to take the game to their opposition from the off, rather than contain and settle for what they'd be gifted. 'Milan are a better team than us,' he admitted through gritted teeth. 'I think we all agree on that – they have better players ... but of course there now comes a point where we want to win.' Referring to their attitude in the lead-up to the first game, he insisted, 'Our attitude is always the same: go and play football; go and enjoy it; try and win.' On a different night, a number of cameo moments from Japanese creator Shunsuke Nakamura would have been enough to catch their opponents unawares, but instead, they had to muster up what courage remained and face Milan at the San Siro, a place which, among other things, was quickly turning into Kaká's playground.

Colin Moffat of the BBC observed that Celtic were 'unlucky' to not get more out of the tie than they did, but I find that fanciful. One thing I will concede is that they should have had a penalty early in the second leg – with Maldini using his arm to bat away the advances of midfielder Jiří Jarošík. It was an uncharacteristically desperate and illegal manoeuvre from the cultured centre-back, and one from which Celtic were unfortunate not to benefit. Other than that, the boys in green had to bide their time and wait for other openings to pose any threat to the Italians, with Milan using every inch of their home advantage to dominate the game's midfield battle. Without context, the late Kaká winner looks to confirm Moffat's view, but it's more an inevitable conclusion to a result they deserved, rather than an awkward end to one they didn't. A display of 'simplicity and maturity' as Ancelotti proclaimed.

The manager also made time to address rising claims that his side had become over-reliant on Kaká, stating that, 'I don't take it as a bad thing when people say we are dependent on his performances,' as it was simply a virtue of 'managing one of the biggest clubs in the world'. That said it was a largely off-target performance against Celtic. It certainly wasn't enough to inspire Ancelotti to believe that his side were favourites to win the whole thing, though he did mention 'a few teams who were considered favourites are [now] out of the tournament', and that if he had to pick one team he'd like to face in the quarter-finals, 'I would say Liverpool.' But first there was a challenge from Bayern Munich to meet.

Bayern's recent success might stand as one of the most efficient and inevitable progressions seen in the game of football. But it's one which unfortunately points to the Bundesliga as an 'inferior league' for allowing such a monopoly to take over. It does, however, highlight Bayern as a machine that earned that position.

From 2012/13 until the time of writing in 2023, no club has threatened their dominance on the domestic league scene. They have ten successive championships to their overall tally of 32 since they were founded in 1900.

They were even gunning for a third German league title three-peat as they faced AC Milan in the quarters of the Champions League. The Bavarians were in search of their fifth European trophy, too. They were a worthy adversary as far as club stature was concerned and a decent match on the pitch.

But for losing Oliver Kahn and having to choose back-up goalkeeper Michael Rensing, the match handshake was a tough one to call before kick-off. Sensing an opportunity to raise some insecurity between the German sticks, Gilardino and Oddo's attempts to warm the gloves of the impromptu stopper were met with staunch defence, all before Pirlo wandered through to head the ball over Rensing and put the home team ahead five minutes shy of the interval.

A disallowed goal and a few misfires after the break were thrust into the limelight in the wake of Daniel van Buyten's equaliser. But Kaká atoned for earlier errors to slide Milan home after winning a penalty against fellow Brazilian Lucio. A jubilant reaction ensued on the San Siro terraces, but was silenced once again by another van Buyten equaliser with seconds remaining on the clock. The Belgian centre-back found himself impressed by the 'self-belief' on show from his team-mates and was brimming with enthusiasm after that late goal – as well as, of course, the two away goals for the return leg in Germany. That being said, he mimicked Ancelotti from the quarters in insisting that in light of Milan's audacious away form Bayern weren't favourites. Milan captain Maldini used similar logic when asked about his team's chances: 'We are here to give our all and are convinced we can succeed,' he said confidently. 'We could have travelled to Munich with an advantage; [but] the advantage is with Bayern. At this level, you pay a high price for mistakes, but that does not ruin our chances of going through to the last four.' Provided they'd be able to learn from their errors and manufacture a cultured response.

Sensing that Milan may have 'tired themselves out', rotation was required by Ancelotti to avoid a similar issue in the second leg. Inzaghi proved a critical inclusion – as he usually did – to combat a talented Bayern side driven to put on a show for their home crowd.

Bayern featured a number of notable stars – most of whom still have club hero status today. Philipp Lahm, as a blindingly bright example of the type of career great players could forge for themselves in the Bayern machine, was a player of incredible talent, evidenced not least by his maturity and versatility. I've said before that Milan's Jankulovski was adept at playing in a number of different positions, but I don't think he or most other players could be regarded as proficient right across the board as Lahm. Central midfield, a deeper middle role, right-back, centre-back. The perfect guy to have. As was Bastian Schweinsteiger for similar reasons.

Earlier in his CV, the eventual Bavarian legend was a nippy, exciting, fleet-footed, attacking wide-midfielder. Over time, his youthful exuberance retreated to make him a simpler, more cultured central midfield player – often taking up a role that led to the aforementioned Lahm having to vacate before finding his home as a full-back. Even since retirement, the pair's bromance is everlasting and stems back to a match against Lens in November 2002 where they both made their senior debuts. Even when Schweinsteiger did leave for Manchester United in 2015, Lahm regularly professed a desire to lure his friend back to the Allianz Arena to end his career in 'the appropriate manner'.

Similarly with their strikers – Lukas Podolski and Roy Makaay. Two outstanding goalscorers who came into Bayern Munich colours with the pressure of having to pick up where they'd left off previously with their former clubs, and had coped fairly well under the pressure. Podolski enjoyed a meteoric rise at Köln before Bayern came calling, and thrilled the fans with his pace and dynamite in his left boot. Makaay was able to feed off the scraps to put away more routine opportunities with ease – somehow leading him to eclipse his eye-watering return for Deportivo in Spain.

If the threat of youth wasn't enough to worry about, Kahn's mature reappearance in goal formed a wholly different proposition to Rensing. Arguably Germany's greatest ever goalkeeper (certainly their angriest), the presence he possessed was a reassuring factor for his team-mates and an intimidating one for the opposition. Ancelotti already mused that Bayern were a 'tough team to break down' without him in the team, and he would improve on their already-stellar organisational skills and 'excellent defence'. But possessing Inzaghi – 'an extraordinary striker [who] lives for European games' – could prove to be the ace up Milan's sleeve.

Losing Schweinsteiger late in the build-up to the match rendered it a pure midfield affair, which Milan appeared determined to claim from the first whistle. Relying on their 600-plus appearance experience in European contention, Ancelotti's men were unfazed as a deafening Bavarian crowd shadowed their every pass in the early stages. Ambrosini and Pirlo in particular were masterful at containing the atmosphere with one or two more touches than necessary to quell Bayern's growing ambition. Seedorf was given the freedom to attack open spaces in front of him, and was a useful outlet when advancing deep into Bayern's half as the game developed. He also moved infield to support his team-mates and cause an overload in that area with Kaká assuming his position on the flanks. Such movement proved instrumental in carving out Milan's first goal after 27 minutes, with the Dutchman latching on to a jink and lay-off from Kaká to twist and face Bayern's goal before unleashing a low, driven attempt from just inside the 18-yard box.

Another lapse in concentration was pounced on by Seedorf a few minutes later, in a move which saw him flick the ball with a reverse pass to send Pippo Inzaghi through one-on-one. Kahn's aggression launched him further off his line than necessary and the striker's mind was made up before he even travelled into the penalty area. In a moment, the net rippled with a confident effort barely evading the crossbar. Milan remained on the retreat to preserve their lead – which they did.

A series of attacking German substitutions were met by defensive movements on Ancelotti's part, whereupon the match began to centre on who could keep the ball best. Both Seedorf and Gattuso had run themselves into the ground before the fourth official's board extended an offer of mercy for the final ten-or-so minutes. Ambrosini, Pirlo and Kaká played the full regulation time, while Inzaghi's exit to make way for Serginho made Milan impenetrable until the end. It was an exemplary show of experience and game management from the Italians, and even their usually reserved manager struggled to contain his excitement in the aftermath. 'I think this was a great performance by my team,' he said with his chest pressed firmly into the microphone. 'You need experience as well as technical ability to do well in the UEFA Champions League and we are very experienced.' Sir Alex Ferguson, the manager he would now face in the semi-finals, concurred, adding further intrigue to a historically competitive rivalry.

> 'It's not going to be easy [for us], but they know it's not going to be easy for them either. I think we have an outstanding chance.'
>
> *Sir Alex Ferguson prior to facing Ancelotti's Milan in the 2007 UEFA Champions League semi-final*

Manchester United were in the latter stages of a transition which relied heavily on their mature players providing guidance and reassurance to their junior talent, all of which proved influential when Ferguson's men dismantled another Italian side in the quarters; sparing Ancelotti's blushes in the process. I remember this game well. And the wonders of modern technology and United fan melancholy ensure that I won't ever forget it, either. My dad and I regularly make it our mission to watch as many games as we can together. We both lived for Champions League nights and on this particular occasion, we didn't know how to approach the game's preamble. United had never won a tie in this competition after trailing from the first leg, but the goal in a 2-1 defeat at Roma gave us hope for the match at Old Trafford, a stadium dubbed a 'fortress' with Sir Alex in charge. Astonishingly, Roma succumbed to a 7-1 defeat. It was arguably their most dominant and unexpected performance in Europe.

Sir Alex could barely contain himself in that post-match interview, and was overawed by the collection of personal stand-out performances he'd watched from his coming-of-age team. Not only was he impressed by 'the speed of our play' and thought the penetration of their movement was 'absolutely superb', he also thought that 'the quality of our game was so high that once we scored two or three, we thought there was going to be something big here'. It was a relentless, merciless performance which typified everything that would turn out to be great about this version of Manchester United. It was a warning for Milan. 'This points the way ahead,' Sir Alex continued,. 'Two years ago [referring to losing a shut-out against the Italians along their route to Istanbul] Wayne Rooney and Cristiano Ronaldo were young boys, but tonight they played like men.' They would both make telling contributions in the first leg against Milan.

Choosing to stick with the same squad which lined up against Bayern in the 2-2 draw, Milan found a makeshift defence proved a chink in United's armour though their weaponry prevailed on this particular occasion. The game plan was clear from United's perspective: a back four of O'Shea, Brown, Heinze and Evra, though relatively unfamiliar, were compact and mobile, but required additional support from midfield against the overwhelming directness of Milan, who knew how to pick their moments and go for them better than any side they would have been up against that season. Darren Fletcher, though not technically as gifted as either Michael Carrick or Paul Scholes, was employed as a marshal to screen the defence and intercept Kaká whenever possible. They did their best to contain the brilliant playmaker, but his two goals in response to Ronaldo's early opener sent Milan into the break 2-1 up. Gattuso falling foul to a niggle a few minutes after the sides re-emerged was ill-timed as far as Ancelotti was concerned. He had now lost a key industrial figure in the middle of the park, an area United were reinforcing. Add that to having to continue without Maldini, and the pendulum swung in favour of the home club. Electric as always, the Stretford End of Old Trafford led a chorus pushing their side to take advantage of the opportunity to drop the wounded animal for good.

Rooney's successful conversion over a flailing Dida brought back memories of the Roma rout, and the Englishman led the charge right until the clock wound down. Adding to an eyebrow-raising 12 shots on target, a mix of desperate defending and point-blank goalkeeping preserved Milan's standing in the contest and the Englishman led another late charge. He was supported by a dazzling Cristiano Ronaldo, chopping and turning his way through whichever defenders were left, and there were a couple of cool, cultured heads in midfield to slow things down and create openings. It would be one of the elder statesmen, Ryan Giggs, who provided the assist for Rooney's late effort. England's 'Golden Boy' from 2006 unleashed a fierce, unexpected thrash at Dida's near post and United went into the second leg 3-2 in front.

Rooney has since revealed that this 'no-holds-barred' approach to the second half was encouraged by the manager at the interval. 'He told us at half-time to keep playing, keep going forward and that's what we did.' The instruction was emboldened by the exits of Maldini and Gattuso. The forward also saw no reason to deviate from that game plan for the Milan leg though much of the attention also surrounded Ronaldo, who was well on his way from precocious talent to undisputed superstar.

Maldini's omission from the beginning and doubts surrounding whether some of the others might last the night, offered impetus to the Rooney–Ronaldo duo to counter-attack any pressure coming the other way. But again, there was Inzaghi lurking in the shadows to be let loose on a still-weakened United defence, which now featured a slower, though more competent Nemanja Vidić in the central area. One in a long line of elements comprising what Ancelotti would call 'perfect football' – and what *calcio* fans now remember as '*La Partita Perfetto*' – the perfect match.

This 'evening of dreams' began in earnest with Kaká treating a soaked San Siro to a pulsating run to the byline, before cutting the ball back away from Vidić but tantalisingly beyond an incoming Inzaghi. He used the energy he had preserved for celebration to gee up the already intense Milanese crowd, who sounded their appreciation for his efforts and kept those decibels raised the entire evening. Expert positioning from veteran stopper Edwin van der Sar foiled a Clarence Seedorf effort, before he smothered a Kaká attempt a few minutes later. But he was powerless as the two combined for the opening goal of the night.

An agricultural floater sent in by Pirlo to the corner of United's penalty area found Seedorf bent out of shape with little option but to improvise to keep the move going. His only options were Inzaghi and Kaká, and his hopeful backwards header happened to fall perfectly into the Brazilian's path. Left-footed, knee over the ball, skipping over the wet turf and beyond van der Sar's reach, it was a textbook manoeuvre made to look easy by a player of supreme quality and confidence, a man right at the top of his game. This would be the final goal he would score in Milan's European journey that season, but ten goals is a tally which few would look down upon, and went some way to building his 'authentic' and 'natural' relationship with the fans of AC Milan. He remembers a chant they used to sing: 'We came all this way, we came all this way, to see Kaká score.' 'Every time I hear that song, when I return to San Siro and they sing it, when I watch a video online and they're singing it, it still gives me goosebumps because of all the emotions tied to it.' Patting his hand on his heart and pointing to the heavens with his arm outstretched is an image which has become synonymous with his time at Milan. With every goal scored and every match won, it's a symbol which spoke for itself: 'God, I thank you for everything you've given me. And to Milan, I will give everything I have for you until I can't anymore.' This tie against Manchester United is when the world saw Kaká for everything he was, without question, the most elegant *trequartista* of his generation and the undisputed best player in world football at his scintillating best.

Seedorf's self-made strike was even more remarkable than Kaká's. This time, a strangely wayward pass from Pirlo was poorly dealt with by the United defence, before it ricocheted out to the Dutchman arriving late in the penalty area. Darren Fletcher's was the first in a sea of white shirts desperately rushing to the ball in a bid to prevent Seedorf from getting a shot away, but to no avail. Sidestepping Fletcher and hurdling Vidić's challenge, he steadied himself to rifle the ball into the same side Kaká found 20 minutes earlier. It was 2-0 Milan, 4-3 on aggregate, and all that was left was for Ancelotti to watch as his men signed off on their humility mission.

Inzaghi ought to have put the game beyond doubt before the break, but he snatched at the chance. Meanwhile, Rooney cut a frustrated, unserved figure at the other end, not helped by a 'disappointing' Ronaldo whose petulance didn't wash with Sir Alex.

For fresh legs' sake, Alberto Gilardino came on for Inzaghi and latched on to a cultured Ambrosini sweep to place the cherry atop this perfect cake. Further substitutions involving Gattuso and

Kaká gave both a chance to savour a moment of appreciation from the stands. An honourable mention for Ambrosini too who, assist aside, carried the crunching Gattuso mantle with ease whenever United's brighter players invaded Milan territory. Few of them would have forsaken Dida for taking a seat for the second half, as Ancelotti's Sacchi-esque free-flowing midfield masterclass produced a turnaround few would have expected.

'At the start of the season I said that getting to Athens [where the final would be held] was a Utopian dream,' reflected Ancelotti. 'But now this dream is becoming a reality' for a side that 'showed great unity through the tough times' and could now feel confident about their objective. In search for a reason to explain how his side fell to *I Rossoneri*, Ferguson resorted to superlatives: 'stupendous, fantastic and extraordinary' was how he described a performance that was 'one of the best in their entire history'. He went on to reveal the details of an intimate conversation he'd had with Ancelotti. 'I told Carlo at the end of our semi-final that there is no way he can now not win this competition.' Apparently, Ancelotti had gifted him a 'magnificent bottle of wine' at the game's end, but once he'd sensed that the Scot might not be in the mood for a tipple, he suggested Ferguson drink it without him whenever he pleased. 'I told him I would only drink his wine once I see him lifting the Champions League.'

It might seem strange that a losing manager would be so gracious in defeat – United themselves hadn't reached a final since 1999 and few would have the forethought to wish their opponents well while still reeling from the own loss. That said, both Sir Alex and 'Don' Carlo shared an enemy in the shape of perhaps the only club in the world that was hated by both United and Milan fans: the Istanbul miracle-workers themselves: Liverpool Football Club.

CHAPTER FOURTEEN

'Revenge is Sweet'

'I believe in destiny and you can't lose a
final the way we did [in 2005] without
being given a second chance.'

Carlo Ancelotti

I DON'T believe in destiny. But a situation
like that which happened in 2007 threatened to
disrupt that. Milan had been punished at domestic
level, and found time against them as their aged,
depleted squad was given a tougher run than two
years before. Injuries aplenty but they simply never
gave up. Many moments of individual brilliance
and collective togetherness dragged that proud red
and black strip to the final. Sensible business in
the summer, and winning the Community Shield,

set the tone for what was a very impressive season for Liverpool. Pantomime figures such as Djibril Cissé, Djimi Traoré and Florent Sinama-Pongolle were swapped with experienced, dependable replacements. Dirk Kuyt was one. An Inzaghi-esque poacher with a knack for popping up where his opponents could not predict, he arrived off the back of some stellar form for Feyenoord and would wear that 'cult hero' tagline with pride come the end of his six years on Merseyside. Craig Bellamy was an acquired taste, but suitable to this boisterous team. Jermaine Pennant was a risk, but a calculated one when his age and potential was factored in. But above them all was the tenacious Argentina international, Javier Mascherano.

The Reds had won the race for the coveted midfielder's signature, albeit on loan, midway through the season. Even then, the deal wasn't without complications. This time, instead of those pesky third-party ownership regulations blocking the move before it could get going, it was FIFA's view on how many clubs a player was allowed to represent in a 12-month period. The cap was two, but Mascherano had already played

for Corinthians, in Brazil, and West Ham United.
Now Liverpool wanted to play him.

After a period of bending the rules Liverpool
were finally allowed to register their new man
in February 2007. Better than that, considering
that neither of his two previous teams were in the
Champions League, he was free to represent the
Reds in Europe, and was determined to do so for
his new manager. 'Benítez lifted me out of a dark
hole 20 metres underground and put me up on a
high,' Mascherano recalled when signing. While
the manager – to whom the Argentine refers as 'a
great person and a teacher as a coach' – theorised
that Mascherano's tough introduction to English
football would help him cope with the expectations
at Anfield. 'He has had six months to acclimatise
to life over here ... and he'll be a bit more used to
things now. Now we will see if he can progress
and improve.' The Spaniard also had a very
specific job description in mind for Mascherano.
With Dietmar Hamann having being sold in the
summer and a void at the heart of his aesthetic
midfield, Mascherano brought a level of industry,
integrity and consistency to a team that wouldn't

have been as successful without it. Together, the midfield triumvirate of Mascherano, Alonso and Gerrard was enough to even make Ancelotti turn green with envy, and they only grew in cockiness as the season passed by.

From open play Liverpool only conceded three goals throughout the knockout rounds. Two of them came from Barcelona but after losing 1-0 at Anfield goals from Riise and Bellamy anaesthetised the sting of losing at home. PSV put up little fight in a one-sided 4-0 aggregate win before Liverpool met Chelsea in a *déjà vu* semi. With the aggregate score at 1-1 a tense and exciting embrace of a penalty shoot-out drove a rapturous Anfield crowd to ecstasy, jeering and waving their London visitors out of the door for the second time in three years. Milan waited on neutral territory. Unlike two years previously Milan were weaker and Liverpool were stronger and Benítez was better placed than most to overcome Ancelotti's plans. But Ancelotti had another trick up his sleeve to inject much-needed team spirit into his unsure bunch. A winter training camp gave confidence to a side Ancelotti admitted were rocked by the news of the summer. 'We wanted to forget what had happened last August,' he explained – 'the bad performances and the docked points.' That being said: 'I think we worked very well in Malta.' One of the dilemmas Ancelotti had to solve was whether to pick Gilardino or Inzaghi at the point of his attack.

On the one hand, Gilardino is 'very good in the fast counter-attacks and in one-on-ones'. On the other, 'Inzaghi is more of a finisher [who] has experience in finals,' and was a player they could have used in Istanbul and who was probably champing at the bit to have an influence this time. This gave Pippo the 'psychological' edge to start, with the rest of the squad needing little intervention.

For a match like this 'experience counts for a lot' so Paolo Maldini's return from injury was of almost incalculable importance, not just for his obvious defensive ability, but also for his intangible qualities as a scorned captain with his eyes set on a fifth European title out of a possible eight, as the walls of retirement closed in. Postponing treatment for a knee injury to be ready, Maldini hobbled into his unconventional role as a centre-back alongside

Nesta. Neither of them was quick but both were masters in the art of 'trying to not make a mistake in the first place'. Tasked with forcing errors few could see, Benítez selected Dirk Kuyt, whose penalty had ended the semi-final against Chelsea, as his lone striker.

Only one season into his Liverpool career, the hard-to-catch Dutchman found his spiritual home on Merseyside under Benítez's tactical discipline. 'He prepared us for everything,' he said. He also would not be the only one in the squad who would relish the opportunity for a second edition of that 'great, historic match' in Turkey, from which only five of the heroes survived for the rematch.

Steve Finnan stayed at right-back despite the pressure of a young Álvaro Arbeloa, John Arne Riise regressed to a defensive position on the opposing flank, and Jamie Carragher – fresh from signing a new contract on the eve of the match – maintained his station at centre-back. Usual partner Sami Hyppiä's injury problems throughout the season allowed a positive run of form for newcomer Daniel Agger, of Denmark. The Dane had taken a little longer to harden to the task of being a Liverpool central defender. His aerial timing needed work, as did his positional sense in adjusting to a quicker game. But his ability on the ball and eye for the occasional strike on goal was a proposition too interesting to turn down. A superb curling effort in the second semi-final leg versus Chelsea followed his inaugural thunderous blow from afar to sink West Ham at the beginning of the Premier League season. It wouldn't be top of his job description, but it was an unconventional quality for a central defender to have. On coming to Liverpool he was an easy target for Premier League players aiming to make the Dane lose his cool. But he learned to harness his temper and create opportunities to prove how good he could be. 'I actually like criticism,' Agger said. 'If someone says "that wasn't good enough" and that I played poorly then, next time, I try and prove something to them … it helps me.' Benítez kept faith with his new defender but hedged his bets with a Mascherano-shaped insurance policy in midfield.

Ancelotti did himself no favours as he added fuel to the tempestuous Argentine's flame in the build-up to Athens; citing him as a suitor for their appearance as a 'Mediterranean type of team' which lacked 'the DNA of the English'. Apparently, this was intended as a compliment by the Italian who later appraised Liverpool as being 'very organised and with an extraordinary capacity for concentration'.

With Mascherano's protection, Alonso and Gerrard's reassignment in midfield allowed both to flourish, with the former looking to put earlier injury troubles behind him and to cement his reputation internationally after representing Spain at the 2006 World Cup. This, the harrowing Istanbul equaliser and even a few half-pitch strikes that would have even Agger scratching his head, highlighted Alonso as a man to contain should Milan have any hopes of restoring their good name. Similarly, Steven Gerrard wasn't to be given an inch, or he'd take a mile.

The decision at the interval two years before to move Gerrard in behind the striker was an inspired move by his manager, and this time he would be in that position from the start. This time he seemed to back his team-mates more than the fortuitous bunch who were 'even shocked ourselves by what we achieved' having already accepted that 'we were not necessarily the best team in Europe'. This time 'it's been a different feeling all the way through'. That underdog mentality had been replaced with a belief that they deserved to be where they were and were entitled to go all the way. 'We've come on so much as a team and don't see reaching this stage as a bonus anymore,' Gerrard candidly explained. 'I actually expected us to be challenging to win it … over three years in Europe we have played all the best teams and come out on top. That tells you how good we've been.'

By this point, Gerrard's football IQ had vastly improved. That youthful exuberance and natural desire to venture forward had assumed a more cultured form as the years went by. Just one week shy of his 27th birthday the world saw glimpses of the cross-field passing, crunching tackling, eye-of-the-needle passing from Gerrard we had come to know and love. He was still involved in goals but not so much as he dropped further into midfield. But in Benitez's later years he was allowed a free-form role in behind the striker. It could be argued that the Liverpool manager tended to rely too much on his captain just as many accused Ancelotti of doing the same with Kaká. Such was the depth of Gerrard's qualities that many predators attempted to lure him away from Anfield. They included – perhaps most famously – José Mourinho's Chelsea. The Portuguese twice attempted to steal the Scouse hero from of his hometown club with sly digs at Benítez's mismanagement providing a mind game with no end product. Perhaps less famously, was a light approach made by Ancelotti himself.

Even he was a little hazy on the details, though the timing suggests he professed an interest in Gerrard sometime between the two Champions League finals – reasoning that 'it would have been fantastic' to pair him with Andrea Pirlo. Bemoaning the 'unbreakable bond' Gerrard had with Liverpool acting as the stumbling block in a negotiation that never truly advanced beyond initial interest, he'd even consulted Pirlo with regards to a potential deal to see how it would be received at his end. 'Without any hesitation I told him "do it – go and sign him."' Pirlo had no issues with a midfielder he considered 'the most complete in Europe'. Praise cannot come much higher than this for Liverpool's danger man.

With that in mind, Ancelotti chose to further the story of his side's relentless dependency on Kaká with greater defensive presence in his midfield. Gattuso and Seedorf were another two of the six outfield players to overcome symptoms of 'Istanbul Syndrome' to be declared fit in 2007, but with Kaká's station mimicking that of Gerrard's behind Inzaghi, it revealed an Ambrosini-shaped slot in behind that only he was equipped to fill. The Italian's career was generally predicated on his desire to give his all for the badge, and he'd rarely been found wanting. Ambrosini, who had missed the 2005 final through injury, was thus presented with a rare 'second chance' that he was determined to put to good use.

Echoing Gerrard's sentiment, he agreed that 'Liverpool are even stronger [now] than they were last time around ... they are very well managed and well-organised, and they have some important individuals in the side.' Suffice to say, Carragher and Alonso from the last match would have been fresh in his mind, as possibly would be

Mascherano, who saved most of his best football for the Champions League. Yet Ambrosini also continued Milan's focus on Steven Gerrard – whom he ventured was the 'greatest midfielder in Europe' at that time ... ahead of Kaká! Nonetheless, the multi-functioning box-to-box man refused to cower under the prospect of having to match and contain Gerrard. In fact, he thought it 'enormously satisfying to pit my wits against him', something he called a 'great buzz' during match week as the two men prepared for the midfield battle, the game's most hotly anticipated contest, and arguably the most pivotal in deciding the outcome.

Wingers Jermaine Pennant and Boudewijn Zenden paired well against Marek Jankulovski and Massimo Oddo, with concentration being the key to ensure that an uneven ricochet didn't allow the mercurial Englishman to pace his way to the byline, or for the cultured Dutchman to add to the central midfield numbers and push the others further forward into the Milan penalty area.

With both sides opting for a single striker, movement was always going to be key. Maldini's age and Nesta's intelligence would in theory force Kuyt to play mostly with his back to goal with few chances predicted to come from runs in behind, whereas the evergreen Inzaghi might hope to capitalise from some ball-playing exuberance from Agger or a mis-step from Carragher leading a higher line to get into his favourite one-on-one position against an inexperienced José 'Pepe' Reina.

Mirroring formations shifted the importance of the game's fate to the midfield battle where, interestingly, neither manager appeared to dwell on the other's choice. Instead they prioritised their own versions of the game plan to bring out the best from their players. Side-by-side, it's difficult to pinpoint exactly who would be accountable for which opponent. Facing Zenden, snarled Gattuso. Opposing Pennant, stood Seedorf. Against Kaká presumably it would have to be Mascherano – much like Gerrard versus Ambrosini. But then that would leave Pirlo and Xabi Alonso. Perhaps theirs was a purists' affair to see who could play better in regulation time. At least, one would hope. But whatever the theory, reality proved that this game would not begin or end with the technical ability of one player over the other. It was a test of character, a spectacle of belief and a tale of redemption only one side would want to remember. Burdened with two chastening years on the wrong side of history, an era-defining 90 minutes lay ahead …

> 'It really did feel like it was my last chance. Not only for me, but for that whole generation in the team. It was a once in a lifetime opportunity.'
>
> *Paolo Maldini*

Milan were fighting for their name, to celebrate and preserve the memory of their latest great, golden generation of players who deserved more than to be plagued by the Istanbul trauma.

Despite the pressure and the balance of power in favour of the opposition – when it came to age, squad balance and empirical belief – Milan possessed an intangible drive to correct the sins of the past. You could see that weight bearing heavy on their shoulders as that famous Champions League anthem echoed through the terraces of the Olympic Stadium.

In a bid to elevate their dwindling reputation after revamping the old European Cup, UEFA tasked British composer Tony Britten with composing a timeless piece worthy of bringing a unique sense of occasion for the new Champions League. Along with the commercial redevelopment of the Premier League in 1992, the football world was venturing into unknown territory and this iconic piece of music which started as 'just another job' for Britten, translated into a simple, yet elegant summons to Europe's elite.

As the Academy of St Martin-in-the-Fields chamber orchestra sent the new work soaring into the air above Athens the cameras panned from left to right to paint an all-too-familiar and painful scene for the *Rossoneri*.

Slowly, the operators filmed through a relaxed Liverpool squad, with Dirk Kuyt and Jermaine Pennant even finding time for some nonchalant mid-anthem conversation. Liverpool faces became more serious as the camera made its way along the line. Finally the camera zoomed towards the Liverpool captain, whose rallying cry rang fresh in the ears of his team-mates: 'We do not want to leave Athens upset and with regrets that we have not brought the European Cup home,' he said before the walkout. 'We want to make history, be heroes and come home as winners.' That being said, the Englishman was reticent to dismiss the challenge of the weakened men in white who 'will feel they have something to prove after the way they caved in' before. The deadpan approach adopted by almost every Milan player before the pre-match handshakes suggested they – with the exception of a jittery Inzaghi trying to control his nerves – were singing from the same hymn sheet.

Whatever Maldini was staring at, he didn't break character, and the rest of his defenders followed suit. The comical height difference between Jankulovski and Dida failed to capture the broad Brazilian's face as he looked to cast his former errors into the abyss; to which *GOAL* refers as one of the 'costliest goalkeeping errors in football history' in their written archive. He, like many others, would seek revenge in Athens and was determined to win that trophy 'at all costs'.

A faint smile on 'Ricky' Kaká's face banished whatever few voices of doubt sprung up regarding his mental fortitude for the night ahead. Pirlo and Nesta looked as though their minds were elsewhere and then, we had Clarence Seedorf. The Dutchman had already won the trophy twice and was now going for an unprecedented third.

Reflecting on the match in an interview with UEFA in 2019, Inzaghi revealed his inner monologue as that fabled theme blared through the Olympic speakers in Greece that night. 'Inside I said to myself that if destiny has given me the opportunity to play a game I couldn't play before, against the same team, it probably meant I was going to score. Destiny wants me to be the star.'

Before any player could think themselves into a state of panic, both sets wheeled away to set up for what was to be one of the most thought-provoking ends to perhaps Europe's most fascinating fixture. England vs Italy. The Mighty vs The Fallen. Liverpool vs AC Milan. To the victor, goes absolutely everything.

Liverpool kicked things off from right to left, quickly forcing the ball out wide to Pennant as an early indication of their tactic to isolate Milan's full-backs with their wide midfielders instinctively coming infield to suit their natural understanding of that region. The early pressure was dealt with. Pennant looked menacing but struggled to make much headway in what was looking like a cagey affair before the ball broke to Kaká in the 16th minute.

Jankulovski advanced into the Reds' half before running down a cul-de-sac and retreating with his head held aloft to see who was worth picking out in the centre. There, he found Kaká with a hopeful toe-poke into his chest. Mascherano, as predicted, offered very little room to manoeuvre and forced the Brazilian magician into a snap shot which stretched Reina to his left.

Gerrard had a similar chance at the other end but sliced the ball before another brash effort from Boudewijn Zenden struck a retreating Maldini and deflected kindly into the path of Xabi Alonso. Memories of Kaká's strike against Manchester United at the San Siro came flooding back as the Spaniard strode into view, before unleashing arguably the cleanest strike of the night thus far. With his instep, he caressed the ball towards Dida's right but angled it just beyond the post. A let-off by his high standards from long range.

It would take another 15 minutes before any real threat materialised for either side, but when it did, both Kaká and Alonso would be involved. Making the most of a scruffy clearance from Jamie Carragher failing to deal with an innocuous Seedorf hook into the box, Kaká took control with his back to goal and found Alonso standing in his way as he looked to pivot. Alsono upended Kaká and the referee signalled a free kick just outside the Liverpool penalty area with under a minute of normal time remaining in the first half.

Seedorf offered his services for the direct set piece, but Pirlo's languid frame soon made him an onlooker like the rest of us. Angled too centrally to offer much purchase to the 'wrong side' of Reina, it would have to be an epic strike for Pirlo to thwart the Spanish stopper; right into any of the four corners. Or it would most likely form a routine save for the Spanish goalkeeper. Unless Inzaghi had something to say on the matter.

'We had a joke that it was a routine free kick, because I scored four goals like this in that season, but obviously it wasn't,' Inzaghi explained later. 'There was an element of fortune about it, but I always tried to take up that position, because I knew Pirlo hit free-kicks that way.' Transforming Johan Cruyff's criticism into a compliment, Inzaghi did exactly what the Dutchman thought he was able to do: being in the right place at precisely the right time. On this occasion, it just so happened to be midway through the trajectory of Pirlo's tame-looking effort toward Reina's left side. Meeting the ball with his abdomen, Inzaghi guided it beyond the flat-footed goalkeeper. He sprinted across the Olympic track to collapse at the feet of the Milan fans, arms outstretched. He and Milan were now halfway through reaching their destiny. It was an all-too-familiar feeling for the boys in white but there was no opportunity for complacency to set in. A 'quiet and calm' Carlo Ancelotti barricaded the doors and adjusted instructions as to how to approach the second half.

'He always understood our state of mind and how to handle us,' said Ambrosini, who marvelled at the stellar man-management qualities of his coach. 'He talked a lot with the players and knew exactly how to transmit his ideas and concepts of the game. He always understood our state of mind and how to handle us.' In this case, Ancelotti knew first hand that tranquillity might be the key, and it was probably best to not say much just to fill the silence if all it did was remind his players how stressful the next hour was going to be. 'Ancelotti prepared us like it was a normal match,' Ambrosini continued. 'For him, if you are playing against a lesser team or in a Champions League Final, it was the same. He wanted the same effort from each game.' It was an extremely simple instruction which helped to cut through the noise of the occasion.

The Milan cavalrymen took their time marching back on to the Greek grass as a restless Liverpool assumed positions ahead of time. They waited for the men in white to kick off and tried to do what they did last time, using fast breaks and direct counter-attacks to inject uncertainty into the Milan defence. But this time Milan held firm, a well-timed poke away from a marauding Gerrard by Nesta in the penalty area setting the tone. As did a caution-worthy challenge on Pennant by Jankulovski.

German official Herbert Fandel flexed his trigger finger over the next 15 minutes, pointing at Carragher and Mascherano who joined Jankulovski and Gattuso on his list of yellow casualties. Clipping the wings of the aggressors ought to have encouraged the creative players to invade their space a little more often but it speaks to the unwavering discipline of both sides that the game enjoyed few clear-cut chances and all men remained on the field until the end.

One of the better chances of the second half fell to Steven Gerrard, pouncing on a lackadaisical piece of distribution by Gattuso to run at Nesta. A brief game of pinball ensued as it bopped and slid between him and the Italian defender before he controlled it and bore down on Dida. On his wrong foot and travelling wider than what was ideal, Gerrard attempted to angle his body the opposite way to caress a shot toward the far post, but he failed to get enough purchase to provoke the goalkeeper into anything more than a routine save. And as if pre-empted by the football gods themselves, while Liverpool's talisman squandered his chance for glory, Milan's would not.

Receiving the ball from Ambrosini on the half-turn, Kaká turned to see a surprising amount of free turf open in front of him. Sensing an opportunity to strike, he took just a single touch out of his feet to assess his options. He could either launch a hopeful strike in the goal's general direction and pray the gods would help him out, or go for the sure thing and see if Inzaghi could be found at the end of his angled run between Carragher and Agger while a tired Riise was playing him onside. Naturally, he chose the latter; prodding the ball toward a galloping Inzaghi with nothing but Reina and geometry standing in the way. Much like Gerrard 20 minutes earlier, he was forced a little wider than he would have liked but the deadly marksman made no mistake. Mirroring Gerrard's effort, Inzaghi took a step further to travel even wider toward the corner flag to unsettle Reina, before sliding the ball underneath him. The Spaniard could not get down quickly enough and the striker wheeled away.

'That celebration was the climax,' he said. 'Running like mad, on my knees, crying. It was a mixture of emotions.' Kaká won the race for first place and was equally exhilarated. He joined his team-mate on the ground before embracing as if they were the only two men in the stadium.

Despite playing in an iconic era for Italian *calcio*, a new-look *Galactico* project for Real Madrid at the Bernabéu and even in three World Cup crusades with Brazil Kaká was overcome, saying 'I remember everything about the Champions League atmosphere'. It was a time so enjoyable for Kaká that he managed to find the light in even the darkest of times. Referring to Istanbul, though it was a 'really tough' thing to deal with, 'It Taught me a lot, it made me grow a lot both as a person and on a professional level.'

The following campaign's semi-final loss to Barcelona in 2006 only sought to compound the misery, leading to usually calm and collected characters like Kaká giving in to self-doubt as to whether they'd be able to reach such heights ever again, or even if their time had been spent. Those two years 'really were difficult' he admitted in an interview with MilanTV in 2021. You could see that raw emotion bared raw in this moment with Pippo. The man looked exhausted as he reached Inzaghi and there were no words to explain what they felt. All they could do was scream, hug and look to the heavens to express their gratitude for granting them this moment. Inzaghi reserved his sincerest appreciation for the manager.

Galliani, of all people, called Inzaghi's fitness into question on the eve of the match and confessed his thoughts to Ancelotti: 'I told [him] that maybe it was better to make Gilardino play instead.' Astoundingly, Pippo agreed. 'I wasn't well,' he said, and now 'had huge pressure on me'. But he found confidence in the attitude of his team-mates who were ready and willing to accommodate his shortcomings. When asked the question which of his colleagues he favoured most, he brushed it off as 'too difficult' before listing the obvious candidates: 'I had Maldini and Nesta, I had Pirlo, Gattuso, Ambrosini, Seedorf, Shevchenko.' But even then, he made time for his hugging partner. 'If I have to name a name, I have to say Kaká, with him we did something extraordinary together.'

With fewer than ten minutes remaining, circumstances forced the usually disciplined Benítez to cast his tactical sensibilities to the side in desperate search of an Istanbul sequel.

Perennial target man Peter Crouch had entered the fray moments before the second goal, and with Harry Kewell, Jermaine Pennant and the overlapping John Arne Riise and Álvaro Arbeloa on either side, service into the towering forward stayed constant to the end. As the clock ticked over, the Australian wide man found his original cross blocked by a white shirt and out for an in-swinging corner. Prior to it being taken, Milan made the switch for Alberto Gilardino to replace Inzaghi in a move which fed into the old adage 'never make a sub before a corner'. The right-footed Pennant struck the resulting corner with purpose in Crouch's direction, but Agger got in ahead to help the ball further toward goal and over Massimo Oddo with Dirk Kuyt waiting by the line. Reacting in a way that would have made Inzaghi proud, Kuyt nodded the ball across goal to bamboozle Dida and bring back old memories. 'Oh no, not again' were the words

Kaká used in an interview with the official AC Milan website. There were just a few minutes of additional time remaining in which to claw back the game, so a Liverpool recovery was much less likely than in Istanbul. But it could yet be done. 'We felt the fear,' Kaká confessed on behalf of the rest of his team-mates and inadvertently for the manager, too. By this point Ancelotti had joined Benítez on the 'anything goes' bandwagon to make sure things didn't slip out of their grasp once again. Kaká called it a 'battle of wills' forced on to the shoulders of his team-mates as a final hurdle en route to redemption. It was a test. And they passed.

Mustering up whatever energy remained to counter the momentum from Kuyt's header, the usual calm and elegance typified by Milan's play was displaced by an unaesthetic, animalistic intent to cling on to what was theirs. Nothing could have taken this title away from them. Naturally Liverpool found it impossible to resist Milan's press and enjoy much freedom in their half to advance upon Dida once more. Until, just before the 93rd minute, reality dawned.

'We have done something incredible. It is
the greatest victory we have had.'

Carlo Ancelotti reflecting on winning the
Champions League in 2007

Greek folklore is not left wanting for authorities on
the concept of overcoming adversity. Socrates – the
philosopher, not the Brazilian midfielder – once
said: 'Falling down is not a failure, failure comes
when you stay where you have fallen.'

Milan did not stay fallen. Plato believed that
'If one has made a mistake, and fails to correct
it, one has made a greater mistake' – a principle
to which this team were determined to adhere.
Finally, there is Aristotle, who hypothesised that
only when one has overcome their fears, will they
ever 'truly be free'. With this achievement, AC
Milan really were free.

That shrill sound of the referee's whistle
provides one of life's greatest dichotomies. It can
make you smile or it can make you cry. There's
rarely an in-between reaction.

Only two years ago, that very sound signalled
Andriy Shevchenko to step forward and take
that fateful spot kick in Istanbul. At the same

time it sparked Jerzy Dudek into action and only one man could come out on top. Then, before the echo had time to dissipate throughout the stadium, it was replaced by a roar loud enough to mock the *Milanisti* as they streamed out. Now, instead of crushing to the ground with tears in their eyes as an army of red marched on to their territory, the men in white rejoiced. Not so much in vengeance but in pure, unbridled self-satisfaction. Especially for the players who had played in both finals.

An excessive number of painkillers were apparently to blame for Maldini's hazy recollection of events but in typical Milan fashion, his team-mates were around to lighten the burden. Now-three-time UEFA Champions League winner Clarence Seedorf credits the Athens story to the 'hard work' and 'great spirit' shown by him and his team-mates throughout the competition. Kaká went one further to describe this team as a 'beautiful side' that deserved this Greek experience. Gennaro Gattuso couldn't help but growl at the memories which helped to fuel his own performance, which he said 'will stay with me for a lifetime, but this is a different story'. While 'SuperPippo' (as he may now be called) said 'these are the evenings that remain with you for all your life', having found it a little easier to cast the past away without actually playing in it. Another sidelined, though very much prominent member of this Milan dynasty, Silvio Berlusconi, was overjoyed at the efforts of his manager and players for repaying his faith and reclaiming their title as European champions. As for the manager, he aimed to shift the focus on to the collective resilience and maturity of his team for working their way through a treacherous knockout journey. How, in the city of ruins and following their own ruinous preparation to a season which countered them at every turn, they somehow found what was needed to piece their esteem back together.

Despite it being 'the most difficult year since I have been with Milan', Ancelotti pointed to 'great harmony' between himself and the club as the underlying factor which absolved them of the scandalous summer they were ordered to endure. 'We never looked for an alibi or to blame anyone,' and in fact their resulting strength and togetherness was born out of having little option but to 'face our problems and solve them'. He hoped this would be a beacon of inspiration to other clubs who may find themselves in a similar position, as well as a positive representation for the dwindling reputation of *calcio*. Eventually, Ancelotti used an interview for a positive comment about his own contribution, but even then, it was a love letter for his employer. 'We never lost sight of what we wanted to achieve [and] what I've achieved is due to the fact that I feel I belong to Milan. I wore this shirt as a player, and winning important trophies wearing the shirt makes my feelings and relationship with Milan strong.' Overshadowing Inter's domestic title win would have been the cherry on top of the cake for him too, I'm sure.

The story should end here. They did it. Even when everybody thought they were incapable and 'past their best', they stared into the eyes of the ghosts of their past and lived to tell their tale. Now would surely be the time to grow old, reflective and grey, slumbering in their rocking chairs hoping for a wistful youngster to ask what it was like 'in the olden days.'

But they still had one more peak to conquer. As if Europe wasn't enough, the heralded era of this fabled club left no stone unturned. Next up: the world.

CHAPTER FIFTEEN

'The Best Team in the World'

BY THEIR own admission, FIFA are pretty proud of their Club World Cup product. A quick visit to their website confronts the visitor with a brazen, emboldened tagline stating that its purpose is to bring together 'the best domestic talent from across the globe' in a mini-league to determine who's 'the best of the best'. So, in a bid to end this unquenchable thirst of football fans the world over to align their team with this definition, FIFA obliged with a simple proposal: bring the two best clubs from the two most reputable continents in the world and have them fight to the death for the special honour to be called 'world champions' at club level.

This proposal was the brainchild of then-CONMEBOL president José Ramos de Freitas who, having noticed the momentum being gathered by UEFA's newly formed European Cup competition in the mid-50s, worked together with the European secretary-general Pierre Delaunay to set up a grudge match between the winners of the European Cup and CONMEBOL's equivalent Copa Libertadores. As is usually the case with these things, the necessary movement of change faced the immovable force of age and tradition before the game progressed. It took two years before the CONMEBOL representatives decided it would be in their best interest, and agreed with Delaunay's suggestion which required them to fashion a club tournament of their own to present a worthy and relatable rival for Europe's equivalent. By 1960, the Copa Libertadores was born, along with the winners' right to compete in a mid-season affair called The Intercontinental Cup.

In hindsight, perhaps the turbulent 60s might not have been the most suitable moment for the inauguration of something so celebratory, with political unrest and fan misconduct prevalent throughout the world. Scheduling was also an issue. With many clubs digging their heels in the sand, unwilling to compromise their league duties, for a 'nothing fixture' requiring two games' worth of time to crown the winner of a competition that bore little or no relevance in their pre-season goals. Twenty years on, and with the level of support waning, the timely intervention of a steady corporate sponsor and ridding themselves of that annoying two-leg final system brought this product the stability it needed.

By the 90s, Japan became this trophy's spiritual home and the domestic intrigue presented a vocational opportunity for the teams involved. Over time, the seriousness with which the teams approached this trip grew, and culminated in perhaps its greatest (and most memorable) final in the year 2000. Utter the name Juan Roman Riquelme in front of any Boca fan, and they'll happily rewind the tape.

Suitably charmed by the idiosyncrasies of the tournament, FIFA tried their own iteration of Delaunay's concept, but faced similar issues with a much greater fallout around the same time as that famous Boca win over Real Madrid at the turn of the millennium. Their media investors had gone bust by 2003, and they had to twice postpone the first edition of their new final, but returned with a redefined, more inclusive setup. From this point on, a representative of each region within FIFA's confederacy would be granted an opportunity to work through a knockout tournament and only the two remaining clubs would fight for the honour of their continent. Finally, in 2005, the world said 'goodbye' to the Intercontinental Cup and welcomed the FIFA Club World Cup with open arms, Milan more than most as they had a score to settle from when they last appeared in this battle of philosophies in 2003.

Football is the ultimate embodiment of culture. Much like a dance or class of music it seeks to represent the community it so desperately aims to entertain. Europe prides itself on its sophistication and class, as a self-serving, self-effaced display of everything that's good and modern about the world: home to academia and art. South Americans are unbridled in their imagination and passion for what they love. Expressions of love in its more visceral form. As we peek beneath the surface, we see that football gleefully adopts these inhibitions.

Both at domestic level and even, at times, on an international scale.

The mid-2010s Spain side transported us into the evolutionary world of *tiki-taka*. True connoisseurs would have painted the clear and obvious line to Cruyff's *Dream Team* and Michels' *Total Football* before. The fact remains that this Spain side was the best of its generation and arguably the greatest of all time. Nonchalantly blowing sides away with enough triangle formations to make the Ancient Egyptians jealous, their game was all about technique, grace and tactical geometry. By contrast, you see real honour, passion and grit at the forefront of teams in countries like Argentina, Brazil, Chile or Uruguay. This can manifest itself in a number of unforgettable moments on both the right and wrong end of the Laws of the Game. The best example of being on the wrong side is perhaps Maradona's 'Hand of God' goal against England in the 1986 World Cup.

Sir Bobby Robson later emphatically discounted the striker's attempt to deify the robbery, and argued that 'the hand of a rascal' was a far more apt interpretation. The purist in me wants to agree with him, but the gall of the indiscretion is phenomenal, too. Opinions converge on the second goal however, which was footballing beauty in its purest form.

Shimmying in and out of the England defenders like large cones during a training session before dropping a shoulder to defy Peter Shilton once again, Maradona's 'Goal of the Century' stands as probably the greatest ever scored in the history of the World Cup.

Together, El Diego alone is the painter for a spectrum of art that encapsulates the footballing identity of his region. Naturally brilliant, frustratingly defiant and utterly intoxicating. That is the Latin way. A difficult fit against the natural sensibilities of the European game, and therefore a fitting attendee at FIFA's crowning ceremony, Boca Juniors, as one of the more successful representatives of South American *futbol* have enjoyed regular participation in the *C*opa Libertadores. Treating their overwhelming support group to six local wins, while halving that tally through affiliated Intercontinental Cup trophies. All the while they held dear their foundational principles that integrity and industry overcomes the 'unnecessary' mystique of more 'attractive' clubs. It's an endearing quality that can lead to inspiring examples.

That weirdly forgettable UEFA Champions League win on penalties against Juventus booked AC Milan's place in the Intercontinental Cup in 2003. Roughly four hours behind, the Copa Libertadores Final of that year saw Boca overcome Brazilian side Santos, once the home of Pelé and Neymar, 5-1 over two legs to square off against Milan in front of 70,000 fans in Japan's Yokohama Stadium.

As far as the forecasters were concerned, it was to have been a walkover for Ancelotti's European champions. They had a core of top footballers who had enough experience and chemistry to overcome the 'less sophisticated' Boca. But that doesn't factor in the intangibles.

Conceivably, one can make the argument of there being contrasting forces in either dressing room which affected the outcome of this event. Both of these clubs are monumental institutions in the game of football, there can be no doubting that. But they're bred from surroundings which would've inevitably taken different views on the importance of the title like the Intercontinental Cup, and the opponents they were facing. There is a clear pound-for-pound chasm in quality between the teams that feature in the preceding Copa Libertadores as there is in the UEFA Champions League. So, having already reached the summit of their historic competition to take home the trophy, there could be a sense of 'what's the point of this, then?' for the Milanese. Whereas the Libertadores was the tip of the iceberg for Boca. So, for Milan: they'd won the European honour and now could get an added cherry on top of an iced, two-tiered cake by defeating Boca. In Boca's mind it was like having two whole new cakes instead of one. It simply meant more to them.

I'm not trying to imply that they 'tried' harder in the match, but I'd say that, for a club which never needed an extra incentive to show pride in their club and fight for everything presented to them, the added bonus of toppling such a huge team like Milan fed more into their souls than that of their opponents. This could all be conjecture but it is my opinion. Milan failed to kick on after their relatively early strike by Tomasson and the rapid response from Boca's Matias Donnet to level the tie five minutes later, with little retaliation to restore their lead from *I Rossoneri*, paints that picture for me.

Ironically, the very thing that played into their hands in the drab European final only months earlier stood against them in Japan. Boca won the penalty shoot-out and that year's right to be called the 'best team in the world' under FIFA's older pretence. Four years on, in a year defined by vengeance and redemption, Milan would have yet another opportunity to salvage their reputation. This time in the same stadium.

Clarence Seedorf's second-half strike in the preceding match against Urawa Red Diamonds sent him and his friends on their way back to Yokohama to relive that 'tough match' from 2003. With a stronger squad this time around and a much clearer goal in mind for the year, Ancelotti was taking no chances with his team selection.

An orchestra reminiscent, though nowhere near as iconic, as the Champions League soundtrack welcomed both sets of players on to the pitch in this mid-December tie in 2007. Boca Juniors wore their classic blue and gold strip, while Milan kept it simple with the all-white livery they wore in Athens. Similarly, their squad wasn't much different either. Their only changes came in defence with Daniele Bonera and Kakha Kaladze starting in place of Jankulovski and Oddo. Maldini took his place at left-back for a swansong appearance as captain in the position he most assumed in his distinguished playing career. It didn't take long before the game sprung into life.

A first-time lob on the half-volley from the wonderful Seedorf found Inzaghi advancing beyond the back line, and he was unlucky to not find the far corner of the net, his shot whistling past the post by a matter of inches before five minutes had ticked by. In the 20th minute Kaká went on one of his trademark journeys through the opposing half before sweeping the ball to Inzaghi for an easier finish. As if it could have been any other way for this pair.

Boca hit back two minutes later with a smart header from Rodrigo Palacio deceiving Dida to level the score, and things were even at the break.

Milan re-started the brighter of the two sides and earned an indirect free kick near the touchline, with Pirlo taking control. This time it would be Alessandro Nesta to profit from the maestro's accuracy; preying on a short game of pinball before it sat up invitingly for a half-volley into the top-left corner. A surprisingly confident drive for a centre-back, though a glittering example of the grace and sophistication he possessed.

A long-range effort from Hugo Ibarra was agonisingly close to levelling the match and Milan had only the woodwork to thank for that. Kaká took this as a warning sign, going directly up the other end to squirm an innocent left-footed jab beneath Caranta. He claimed his man of the match performance with another assist for Inzaghi, and Milan ran out clear winners on the night. The final score was 4-2.

Including the preceding cups, winning this final had brought Milan their fourth 'world' title; overtaking the likes of Real Madrid and Boca themselves in the process. A simply perfect way for a 'very proud' Ancelotti to conclude an 'unforgettable year'.

'It's been such a long and difficult road. I'm happy and proud that we have been able to overcome every obstacle along the way and achieve this success in Japan. We had to battle to get here. But we got a measure of revenge on Liverpool, and on Boca too.'

Carlo Ancelotti after winning the FIFA Club World Cup in 2007

He signed off, almost in a whisper, that 'those bitter memories are behind us'. I can't even begin to imagine the sense of self-satisfaction and pride that would have brought Ancelotti to say that, a man whose tumultuous journey could now finally be read as one of the greatest legacy stories in the history of this magnificent football club. As would his masterful management of a set of players who reserved their own place in Milan folklore.

Dida, once a pariah in an era of great gloved tacticians, was technically the best goalkeeper in world football. Paolo Maldini, a truly magnificent defender in his own right, might have retired much earlier had it not been for Ancelotti's touch, but now he could bow out free of 'any regrets or sorrow' having achieved 'all the things I could ask for in my career'. Similarly, Cafu's shelf life extended dramatically once the manager expressed interest in a late revival. The Brazilian is exceedingly grateful to have been given the opportunity to broaden his footprint in the eyes of *I Diavolo*. Alessandro Nesta proved unequivocally that he was among the world's best during his time under his 'second father' in Ancelotti, who rarely ever felt the need to coach his disciple on what it meant to be a great defender.

Gennaro Gattuso's animalistic legend holds firm under the quality of his team-mates. Andrea Pirlo re-used Nesta's paternal description when thanking Ancelotti for reimagining his career in a way even he once doubted. Ancelotti transformed him into the greatest deep-lying midfield player the world has ever seen. Clarence Seedorf deserves to be spoken of with similar acclaim, as his box-to-box qualities were rare. 'I want to thank God, who allowed me to be here today. I thank my wife, my parents and Milan, the team that allowed me to win,' pronounced Kaká at his acceptance speech for FIFA's Ballon d'Or award in 2007.

'I gave my best and got a Ballon d'Or' said Andriy Shevchenko in an Instagram post when he did the same thing in 2004. And what better way to end than with the incredulous success of Pippo Inzaghi, an emblematic figure of what many wouldn't have believed was possible.

In retaking their place at the pinnacle of the game, they rubbed shoulders with the fabled Milan teams of old, armed with a narrative so inconceivable, it had to be seen to be believed. It was a tale full of heartbreak, destiny and triumph in equal measure. This is the story of Carlo Ancelotti and his AC Milan. Who came, saw ... and conquered all that laid before them.